# Skint Mob!
## Tales from the Betting Ring

*Simon J. Nott*

Simon Nott Publications

First published in 2013
by Simon Nott Publications
Tiverton, Devon, England

**www.simonnott.co.uk**

ISBN  978 0992 7554 09

*Printed in Great Britain by
Imprint Digital, Exeter*

Dedicated to Jack Lynn.

# Chapter 1

*Betting shops, pubs and the bookie barman.*

I had a phone call one evening from a guy called Dave Simms that totally changed my life. Would I like to do him a favour and work at Taunton for bookmaker Jack Lynn? Of course I would and that phone call resulted in twenty years travelling the turf working for bookmakers.

That working life in the betting ring came totally out of the blue. It was down to one guy that had a penchant for beer and skittles. I had been keen on racing and betting since I first ventured into the mysterious world behind the blue and green dangling pieces of plastic of the William Hill shop in Gold Street, Tiverton, sometime in 1982. Being underage it was the fact that I wasn't supposed to be in there that lured me, rather than any interest in horse racing. Apart from watching the Grand National and putting 10p bets on with my Great Uncle who ran Rackenford Post Office there was no family interest at all.

The betting shop was situated across the road from the Tiverton Labour Club (where a 17 year old who looked about 15 could get a pint of mild for 49p, no questions asked), next to the White Horse pub. The hooligan element of town used to drink in there but the landlord drew the line at underage kids. It was a bit scary unless you were escorted into the back bar and protected by one of said hooligans, so the Labour Club it was, for no more reason than the beer was cheap and they sold it to me.

The other thing that attracted me to the mysterious world behind the betting shop door was the fact that it seemed to be a place where extra beer money was easy to come across. People were forever rushing back into the club waving yellow scraps of paper, talking in weird tongues of winning fortunes on things called forecasts, Yankees and Union Jacks. It seemed so easy, just wander in, risk a few quid and wait for the extra funds to come rolling in to fill the Labour Club bar coffers.

Needless to say, I wasn't too good at realising that the average punter only sings when he is winning. Quite a few of them were still in the betting shop late afternoon trying to get their rather large losses back on the last dog race or bumper at some provincial Irish meeting, that often suffered from 'Telephonic interruptions.' That didn't stop people staring at the speaker though. Anyone who had a winning day was generally expected to sub those who didn't. My first bet wasn't too clever either, 50p each-way on Cat-O-Nine Tails. How was I to know that 2-7 wasn't really an each-way price? I just saw that the majority of people in the Sporting Life had tipped it. To add insult to the injury with everyone in the betting shop laughing at my bet, it didn't even win. The comforting thought that at least I had two pints worth of stake money to come back was also dashed.

At that time I was working in a poultry processing plant; I had worked in a timber yard, been a building site labourer and an office junior before my daily rides out to the gate at Lloyd Maunder paid off and I eventually got that job. Bagged it I should say, because being 1982 and having left school with virtually no qualifications the factory was the place to work. Nobody in my circle of friends had gone to university or even college. The few who were on apprenticeships earned pitiful amounts and my previous jobs paid around £40 a week. Lloyd Maunder was where the 'well-heeled' worked, four and a half days a week (Friday afternoons free for pub and punting with cash payment burning a hole in your pocket, if it survived the canteen card games that is) and you took home, (previous danger excepted), about £80 a week.

The job itself varied.You could have it pretty cushy packing chicken pieces into packs chatting the girls up all day. Boring, hanging eviscerated chickens onto lines or racks for a brain-numbing day after day. Horrific and hard, unloading crates of live chickens for a row of Devon's finest 'strong but dim' to hang onto a line that took them to their doom. Worse still, you could be working alongside them. They knew how to squeeze a chicken so that it fired high velocity shit at you. I had initially asked to work out in the killing bay because it was most money and they generally finished work by about 10.30am on a Friday.

I soon realised that sitting talking to the girls was the much better alternative than working with guys that could easily have taken lucrative careers as Troll extras for Lord Of The Rings, had they even thought of making it back then, which they probably hadn't, of course. I was soon back into the office with my metaphorical tail between my legs to admit, with no shame whatsoever, that the Killing Bay was far too much work for me and that I would like a transfer. Using a little bit of psychological skill I also added that the guys out there were much better men than me and I had nothing but admiration for their skills and had no idea how they hacked it day in day out. I noticed the line boss of said bay who had been sneering at me with contempt, mellowed and allowed himself a little smile as he heard this endorsement. He readily agreed that he could manage without me and that I would be better off back with the girls.

The other advantage of being in the much kinder environment of the factory was that you could sneak off to listen to the big races that you were missing. The little orange radio that I had proudly owned since childhood came in very handy for tuning in to when you needed to know who had won the Cheltenham Gold Cup. I wasn't averse to a bit of skiving

3

where racing was concerned either. When the new flat season was imminent I knew that a 'sickie' had to be called for the Thursday afternoon. The Sporting Life Weekender had previewed the meeting and highlighted that the combination of Bill O'Gorman and Tony Ives had a runner called Provideo in the Brocklesby Stakes. Of course I would lose wages not turning up to work but the winnings would cover that. And they did that day; the dream team sprint combination of the day did the job. That horse went on to win 16 races that season and in the process wiped the smiles off the faces of the slightly older and more seasoned punters who had asked me to join in their 'five pound in, winner takes all' ten to follow for the flat. Green as grass, I had no idea of the concept of picking horses that would win through a season; I didn't know anything about class and couldn't tell you the difference between a seller and the Derby. The winner of the Brocklesby would normally be a waste of points but come November I trousered the equivalent of a week's wages. It was a rare success though and only slightly tempered the one-way flow from my pocket to the coffers of William Hill.

My Friday afternoons and Saturdays were spent in the betting shop, though I was what is best described as a complete mug punter, betting from the 11am at Hackney hoping trap 6 would get the day off to a flyer. The dog bets were always after a multitude of multiple bets had been placed. Some I understood, some I didn't, Yankees, Union Jacks, Forecast Doubles and a football accumulator which was quite often the only hope of any sort of return after an afternoon punting. I was the betting shop manager's dream. The selections were picked from the Sporting Life and virtually every race was bet on. Of course by Saturday night I was pretty much always potless.

I was hooked though, on the mysterious ways of the betting shop. Now that I had become acclimatised with the betting shop environment and the ne'er-do-wells that lurked there I was fascinated as to what went on at the other end of the speaker that was so gazed at. Where the odds came from, what the stewards who had your bet's destiny at their mercy just when you thought you had got out of trouble looked like and professional punters. They were the fellows that intrigued me. I knew they existed because the pages of the Sporting Life were littered with adverts telling you about the untold riches that you would have won following their bets last week. Many of these adverts were placed by professional punters willing to share their information with you. Mysterious contacts who were having their biggest bet of the year on horses that had been laid out for the race in question and were expected to win unchallenged.

I also loved looking at the results with the noted big bets in them. Images were swirling around in my head of little gaggles of these professional punters sipping champagne in the members' bar before ambling down to the bookmakers and having 'monkey' bets on. I knew a monkey was £500, because I had asked an old sage who told me all about it. The bookmakers remained a mystery to me because they were never in evidence on the television. The preconceived idea I had of these professional punters was of a guy who lived near the gallops, knew all the jockeys, had a hotline to the trainers and spent most of his life with his head buried in form books. I assumed the latter to be correct but it did baffle me why, because none of the adverts said 'I have sorted one out after spending hours going through the form.' It was almost always information from a person who knew the result before the race but still assumed they'd do it anyway.

There was one guy in the betting shop who always had wads of cash and was hallowed as a pro-punter. He was someone who didn't work but just backed horses for a living. Now that was the sort of life I fancied and became fascinated. Larry was a bit of a paradox. He sort of looked the part, always wearing a long black Crombie, but with pretty worn out trainers. I have been told since that you can always tell someone's true wealth by their shoes, but hey, I was young and impressionable. He could be seen walking about as fast as is possible to do without running, either to the betting shop, or from it back home, to watch the race he had just punted on.

When I watched him from afar he always seemed to win. I got talking to him one day and was invited back to his place to see his betting record and huge collection of form books. The first time I had actually seen them, I was impressed and rushed out to buy my first Haig-Superform book. In my mind Larry was a legend and a hero, a punter who won. At around the same time I sent my hard-earned money off for a little book entitled 'Form Book Analysis' by a guy named M L Midgly. This book was going to unlock the secrets contained within the pocket-sized tome I had just bought and separate me from the rest. The reality of the dream of becoming a pro-punter lay within its pages.

My first glimpse of a real pro-punter came one day totally out of the blue. He didn't look much like Larry. The face that stared out at me from the front page of the Sporting Life was a chap named Barney Curley. The headline said that he had been in trouble with the stewards. The only other image that had struck me like that had been a picture of the young Sun Records era Elvis. Barney Curley scowled out from the page, unshaven with a fedora pulled down over his eyes. I had a racing hero, at least the image.

The fantasy on-course world that I had created in my mind contained lots of 'faces' now with Barney Curley at the top of the food chain but I still had no idea of bookmakers. I was interested though and soon spotted that gents who stood in amongst all the bookies with their tripods when the betting ring was briefly shown were making hand signals. I learned that they were betting odds from the erstwhile John McCririck on the television but was still none the wiser. Then a pub further nodded me the way to the racecourse. I didn't know it at the time, but the young couple that took over the running of the Boar's Head in Tiverton were to eventually change my life. Dave Simms was a larger than life chap behind the bar. He had us all entering ten to follow competitions and spoofing for the change for the round you just bought. He had grown up working for bookmakers. Not only that, he also knew the mysterious tic-tac.

It wasn't long before I had learned the bookies' hand signals off by heart over the bar and a few pints of scrumpy. Without ruining the kudos somewhat, if you knew the way odds went the learning procedure wasn't too hard, in fact it was easy, even with cider. In the process you also got to grasp the bookies slang for a lot of the odds because the slang described the moves, 'half-arm', 'eyes', 'top of the head' and so on. I was totally besotted with all things bookie. Dave's stories of big winning days when his boss had 'gone down the book' with a favourite they didn't fancy. Big bets taken that they couldn't hedge and so on. I was immersed in the tales but had yet to set foot on a racecourse.

Despite there being racecourses 30 miles either side of Tiverton, Taunton and Exeter, the first course I ever set foot on was Cheltenham, the Mackeson Gold Cup of 1983. I do remember being so horrified at the cost of beer that I was prompted to write a letter to the Sporting Life. Such were my 18 year old priorities. I would also like to point out it was published the following week under the heading 'A high price to pay.' The other residing memory was the first bet I had, a horse called Sweet Mandy. Despite Dave's advice about shopping around and looking in the back row for value I distinctly remember running straight into 'Ricky and Son' and having my £5 at 9/4 only to see 5/2 a few rows back, just as Dave had predicted.

It was all academic anyway as Sweet Mandy fell long before the business end of the race. I remember little about the rest of the day, even who won the big race escapes me but I do remember being enthralled by the hustle and bustle of the betting ring and the floor-men rushing around calling bets in. I did understand a bit of the lingo but a lot of it was still foreign to me. I particularly enjoyed standing up by the rails where all the mysterious business was done. There were no prices displayed just sharp-suited guys whispering into the well-heeled shell-likes. The wads of cash changing hands and just the general electric ambiance of it all had me hooked.

I didn't get to go to many race meetings but did attend the Welsh Grand National day with Dave Simms where I was suffering a particularly nasty hangover thanks to trying to keep up with Dave and his mate Peg who could drink cider like water it seemed. It also became apparent that despite a sterling effort on my behalf, I couldn't.

Dave's mum was Mayor of Tetbury at the time. She made me breakfast, it made me go green. Dave ate mine and his. I soon recovered once I got to the racecourse and spent most of my time down in amongst the bookies soaking up the atmosphere. I was totally immersed in racing and bored to death with life in the factory, brain-numbing work, in either cold, wet, noisy or dirty conditions, depending on what you were given to do.

I decided to apply to join the Army. There was no real reason apart from in those days young people from my sort of background didn't go off on gap years, or even had gaps, unless they were enforced as in not having a job, and thus no money. I went along to Exeter to take my intelligence test and a minor medical. I failed, I couldn't touch my toes. Such was my determination that I went home, swam and stretched and within a week was back and managed the feat. That was that then. I was going in the army. All that was left was a trip to

Sutton Coldfield for final selection, which of course I would pass.

Once my future was sorted it became harder and harder to take orders from people who were, let's say in the kindest possible way, generally less than bright and did a job that was mind-numbing. I was going into the army any day soon, it was September and the new college year was starting so I hatched a plan. I could apply for a course at college (make sure as many lessons as possible were in the morning), claim dole money, leave my job. So that was it. Much to the consternation of my mum who I still lived with, I jacked it all in, enrolled at college in an art course and became a professional punter!

Yes you read right, I had read the 'Form Book Analysis' book from cover to cover. While it did explain a little of how to read the form, in truth, it really was just a vehicle for the guy's form systems and flogging them. He kept mentioning stepping stone staking plans but hardly explained them. Luckily Larry was on hand to enlighten and told me about a sure fire staking plan. This plan was so simple if you did it right it was mathematically impossible to lose, you just had to be in the betting shop (luckily Art and English, the courses I had chosen were mainly in the morning). He also showed me the book where he had written down all his bets. The plan was fool-proof and simplicity itself. All you had to do was pick a tipster from The Sporting Life, 'Man On The Spot' was suggested because he was the top man at each course apparently.

All you had to do was back all his selections to win £1 plus previous losses. Two meetings per day, with 15 minute gaps, were the best so you could draw your winnings in time for the next race. Twelve races a day was the norm at the time with six at each meeting. I always bet the first horse to win a fiver so the day's winnings would be worth getting. Bear in mind I was previously only on around £80 a week hanging up chicken in various states from live and scratching to frozen and dismembered. I opened a building society account and vowed to deposit a tenner a day from my winnings. As the booty mounted I was going to raise the stakes. William Hill had no idea that I now had the game sussed and was going to become very rich indeed. Weirdly it never crossed my mind why Larry wasn't doing it, but there again it was for beginner pro-punters surely?

As quite often happens with systems things started very well indeed. Which translates to Man On The Spot was doing very well with a couple or more winners a day at decent odds. The building society book was filling up nicely and I was soon dreaming of being an owner and polishing a top hat ready for Royal Ascot. It wasn't that summer festival, but Glorious Goodwood that put paid to my dreams and taught me a very serious lesson about gambling, losing runs are inevitable. Man On The Spot didn't have an off day but an odd ten or so races. That was all it took for me to lose the cash I had and all the money I had fastidiously saved the weeks previously. I did have the guts to actually follow through with the last bet, character building it was too but I was skint again.

That was a blip in my pro-punting career but although crest-fallen I hadn't given up hope. Those tipsters in the paper kept informing me every week that by not sending my £2 in for the Saturday one horse nap I had missed Ryan Hartley's 8/1 winner. Enough was enough I thought, I am going to get me some of that action. So the next week as soon as I saw the advert I sent my £2 into the address in Newmarket and waited with baited breath. The letter arrived in a small brown envelope on the Friday morning. It was no frills but contained the information required to get the ball rolling in my pro-punting career. It was just a single photocopied, crudely typed sheet of paper containing the name of the horse. The first one was 'Lineman' and it was the bet that was going to separate me from the mugs in the betting shop. No more Yankees, union jacks and trap 6 in the 11am at Hackney but a whole score on the one bet. Sit in the Labour Club with a couple of pints, watch Lineman win at 15/2 and collect.

The plan was then to start with a nice tank of £150 to give the slightly tweaked and refined £1 plus previous losses system another chance to make my fortune. The £20 would be saved and invested in the next of Ryan Hartley's hot tips. Neil, the manager at William Hill did give me a slightly old-fashioned look as I placed the £20 on the desk and asked for the price.

The first part of the plan went well. I let the usual suspects 'waste' their money on the dogs while I had a couple of pints. The racing was on TV. I hadn't told a soul about my good thing. The plan was to give a quiet 'yes' when the horse passed the post. As the time of the race got closer I was getting more and more excited, not nervous. After all Ryan was 'very confident' about the horse's chance, the main worry was getting on at the price, and that I did and felt quite smug and rather proud that I was on the inside of a nationwide gamble. That is what it was. Lineman's price started to collapse, a 'steamer' as the be-whiskered one in tweed and deerstalker on TV called it.

It's hard to describe quite how I felt when the horse ran no sort of race. I wasn't gutted, more surprised. That's how green I was, but Ryan had known about the gamble so I was going to send him a £5 for a series of bets and the odd mid-week special. The bets were not actually too bad and a few winners came in through the letterbox but I soon smelt a rat when almost identically worded adverts for other Newmarket based shrewdies used to appear when Ryan had a bit of a bad run. I couldn't work out why these fellows didn't get their heads together. Undaunted I tried a couple of other tipsters, always staking more than I could really afford, often with a car circled in the 'Auto Trader.' I do remember being gutted that I couldn't rush out and buy that Mark II Ford Zodiac I fancied when a horse called Quickstep failed to win one Saturday. The guy, not Ryan but another fellow I forget the name of, who tipped that one up was a little too early as it did go on to win a few races.

Needless to say, rather than becoming the bane of the bookies I was welcomed with open arms. On my arrival at William Hill, generally as the doors opened, I used to be so proud when Neil the manager used to make me a cup of coffee. You have to remember that back in those days there were no frills in betting shops, not even a coffee machine. I'm sure he was being friendly because he actually found my banter and eternal optimism slightly endearing but didn't really want me going to the independent betting shop down the road either. He often used to say 'What's good today Elvis?' I had picked up that nick-name from my greasy hair and teddy boy clobber I used to wear from time to time. He'd even pretend to listen as he rustled up a coffee.

Of course, only a few weeks into my professional punting career and I was skint. I was keen and studied hard. My bedroom looked like a betting shop but most of it was for show. In those days the betting shops had huge multi-coloured cards featuring the day's dog racing on the walls. I snaffled a couple of them along with a whole host of betting slips and set them up along my desk at home. I had bought some out of date form books that were hardly ever opened just so I had a library like I was sure all pro-punters had.

For a little while, very little, I was living the dream and in a sort of fantasy world. My nights would be spent reading Dick Francis books, and on Thursdays I would be at the paper shop for the newly published Sporting Life Weekender. I would carefully remove the results section but rather than pore over them in the search for the next value winner I would dive into the world of Jeffery Bernard who had a column. I loved reading of his lifestyle of booze, birds and winners. Sunday nights were also a highlight, Robby Box on Big Deal. Robby was a pro-punter, mainly on cards but much of the programme was set in Gil's betting shop. I loved it. The punters there stood and stared at the speaker too. It was a little lower-tech than William Hill because occasionally the telephonic interruptions were caused by Gil's dodgy speaker, corrected with a quick 'thwack' of his broom.

I craved the fantasy life-style and longed to be involved. It was of course hardly aspirational but it was a magical time discovering a whole new world that was in a parallel one to mine, a little bit shady, a little bit disapproved of, but mine. I wanted to look the part too, bought a trilby and a camel coat (I wanted a Crombie, I didn't know it was a Crombie, but the sort that Arthur Daley or Michael Dickenson wore) but ended up with a camel overcoat from my Nan's club book, paying a couple of quid a week for 28 weeks. It wasn't really what I was after, but made me look a bit like a proper punter, didn't it?

Sadly, despite the hat and coat my attempt to join the ranks of these mysterious punters was doomed to failure from the outset. My skill at picking winners may not have been honed but what I lacked in know-how I made up for with courage, albeit foolhardy. Giro day I'd head off to the post office, get my money, pay my mum her rent and then get down to the bookies to sort out a winner or two. A short priced £5 double or sometimes the whole lot, yes the two weeks money I had to live on, on one good thing. I particularly remember having £30 on a horse called (quite aptly) Wing And A Prayer at odds of 4/6. I waited nervously for the race. They were off. Then much to my horror, 'Telephonic interruptions.' The commentary never restarted.

Now one of the weird things about the climate in the betting shop was that although it was all of you against the bookie, none of the other punters wanted you to win. Of course being young and full of bravado I would have to tell everyone what I fancied and that I had balls big enough to back it. They'd all outwardly admire your courage but inside they desperately wanted you to do your money. That particular day I remember the time it took for the result of that hurdle race to come through was agonising. I was praying to hear my number, the people peering at you trying not to look like they were all hoping, maybe weirdly apart from Neil the manager, that it wouldn't be. That day, the horse had won by a distance. The relief rushed over me and my chest puffed out. I had turned my £30 into £50 (minus the £3 tax, paid on of course because it was a cert) just for having the guts to plonk the money down.

It didn't happen like that on a regular basis of course. Much of my time was spent just hanging around in the betting shop getting to know some rather unsavoury, transient and downright dodgy people. One such person had us all enthralled for a few weeks. He was a mysterious youngish man of oriental descent with a bowed leg. He appeared from nowhere and started throwing money on horses in a way none of us had seen, hundreds on horses that were winning and winning at decent odds too, a pro-punter from the Far East? That was something dreams were made of for a young me. I had immediately imagined that he had a host of moles, or at least his bosses did, all over the world and he was travelling the country 'getting on' in betting shops where he was unknown before he was restricted and had to move on. He alluded to that in broken English, but not only that, this guy with money in every pocket was trawling the casinos at night, using a roulette system and winning. I'm sure all that sounds ludicrous now, it even does to me as I type it. In my defence I was a young impressionable chap living in a world of Jeffrey Bernard and Big Deal and was totally taken in.

Really taken in. One day a very fraught looking 'Bobby', as he said he was called, came into the betting shop saying that he couldn't get any money. He had some excuse, I can't remember what it was but the problem was he had a winner. He couldn't say which horse but it was running very soon and he needed to get some money. He had a cheque book but no account. Of course I was willing to help, I said. I had an account at the Nat West. I used to go in there every day with the cheques when I was an office junior. Being extremely gullible I said that if Bobby wrote a cheque out to me I would pay it into my account and then ask one of the nice girls if I could immediately draw the cash and give it to Bobby. That would no doubt put me right in his good books and have me privy to all his hot information which would surely set me back onto the coveted road to professional punting.

Hardly surprisingly when I got to the bank, they looked at me as if I was stupid, which of course I was. As I was stressing that the cheque was from a friend of mine, Bobby came hobbling into the bank and tried to get the cheque back. I left, miffed that my chance of getting in with a pro-punter had been thwarted by 'jobsworths.' As I skulked off he was still arguing with the bank girls. Bobby did pop back into the bookies a bit later on but only briefly. We never saw him again. We heard about him though.

About two weeks later around nine o'clock at night there was a knock at the door. My mum opened it and got the shock of her life. Two burly uniformed policemen had come to arrest me on suspicion of attempting to cash a stolen cheque. I was quite bullish to begin with and assured my mum that I knew what it was all about and that I'd sort it out. Once I got to the police station my attitude changed. Away from the cosy, twee and harmless world of mostly mythical professional gamblers I was in a very real one of international organised crime.

The policeman that interviewed me made it very clear that I was into something I didn't want to be anywhere near. He asked what I knew about 'Bobby.' I told him 'nothing really apart from the fact he was a winning punter who bet at casinos and in betting shops before being moved on.' The policeman, at first thrilled me a bit by saying that my description was pretty much accurate, but that it was for an international crime syndicate. My smile soon disappeared when he asked in a very serious voice if 'Bobby' knew where I lived. He said it was important that I told him because the people we were dealing with were so big and dangerous that it was now in the hands of the Metropolitan Police. I was pretty sure that Bobby didn't know where I lived, but of course Tiverton was a small place and if he was in the Tongs or Triads (my imagination was running wild at this point you understand) it wouldn't have taken them long to torture Larry or someone to find out where I lived.

After a few hours at the police station they realised that far from being involved I was just a stupid naive kid. After all, had my account had any money in it and I had drawn cash on the strength of the cheque, it would have been me who was out of pocket. It transpired that the cheque book Bobby had used was stolen from the owner of a local Chinese restaurant. The police dropped me off at home and warned me to be in touch if anyone approached me about the incident or if I saw Bobby again. That night and for weeks afterwards I made sure that once my mum and sister were in bed I'd go down, chain and double check the locks lest a Ninja come to murder us in our beds. That's how daft I was, like a door chain would stop a Ninja.

Despite all my efforts with dodgy tipsters, form study and being a completely trusting idiot most of the time, I was skint. I was enjoying the English and Art lessons at college but was 19, totally broke and living with my mum when one morning a letter arrived that changed my life more than Ryan Hartley's ever did. In all the excitement I had almost forgotten that I had applied to join the Army. I was in. So on 4th April 1985 I had to go to Exeter to officially swear allegiance to the

Queen and on 9th April I was on a train to Wokingham to join the ranks of the Royal Electrical and Mechanical Engineers. The weekend before I joined was actually the scene of my biggest ever win. The fact that it was around £180 sort of sums up that I was better off going into the army, but it was a nice send off to the military. Browne's Gazette odds on to win the Welsh Champion Hurdle and Rhyme And Reason the Irish Grand National. I have no idea why my mates and I did such a double but it was a good send-off from William Hill. Neil the manager paid me out with a genuine smile.

# Chapter 2

*Life in the Army and pro-punting don't mix – do they?*

I am not going to go into massive detail about my army life, not because if I did I'd have to kill you, but because I'm looking forward to getting on to the tales of the betting ring afterwards. There are one or two memories that spring to mind though that might set the scene and amuse so bear with me.

The first thing that I realised when I joined her majesty's forces was that all of a sudden I was very credit worthy. I immediately set about opening credit accounts with bookies, something I had never been able to do before. I had them all, William Hill, Coral, Mecca, Ladbrokes, Guntrips and PTS if I remembered rightly. The idea never was to stay in the army long, though that idea slightly hit the skids when on the day of signing up we were told that as we were joining the R.E.M.E and the Army was spending a lot of money training us up, the minimum term we could sign for was six years and not the three that I had intended. It was alright though the kindly officer holding the pen assured me, you can sign for six but leave after three, plus, signing for six meant you got paid more money. Result.

Basic training had one or two betting moments; I did win a few quid punting on the classics using my accounts. That was the way forward, the odd phone bet on a certainty to build up my tank. I had decided that when I came out of the army I wasn't going to be a pro-punter but a bookie, a much more sensible idea. I did have a punting drawback very early on though. It was very frustrating at the time and wasn't even on the horses.

Before I left Tiverton I had placed a bet of £15 to £8 on Steve (Interesting) Davis to win the world snooker. The ticket was safely in my wallet. Steve Davis was pretty much invincible at the time. William Hill had made a massive rick going such a big price. They were going to pay for my first leave and I was looking forward to triumphantly marching up to the payout before buying the mug punt locals a drink from my winnings, beer was only 49p over the club don't forget. Of course Steve Davis was in the final against Dennis Taylor, a guy who looked as if his glasses were upside-down. The weekend of the final I wasn't worried at all, in fact I wasn't even watching it even though in those days snooker was widely televised. We had a weekend pass, not to go home but we could sign out at the guard room on the Saturday but had to be back to 'stag on' at night.

The guard room was a pretty austere place. The only comfort, some plastic bunk beds, a kettle with brew kit and a TV. The way it worked was that you had to get your combat kit on and turn up at the allocated time, get inspected, be shouted at and then do two hours on and two off all night. The duties were walking around in pairs with a radio and pick-axe handles each guarding the camp while your mates slept. During the day I had kept half an eye on the snooker. As expected it was all going well, Steve Davis was in fine form, so much so that it looked as if poor old Dennis Taylor was going to be humiliated. The bet was won as far as I was concerned.

It was all change when I got into the guard room after my first two hours. Some of the guys were glued to the TV, the snooker was on and the room was buzzing about an amazing comeback. Well, I knew that was bad news straight away. After being in a commanding position Steve Davis had wobbled and it was all on the last frame. It was OK though as that frame was going the way of my man. He was seemingly on top and cruising when the shout came up from the office 'Stand Up!' We all had to jump to our feet, normally just so that someone could be fingered to complete the very important task of making the usually very bitter corporal or sergeant whose career had resulted in working the depot guard room, a cup of coffee. This time it was just to let us know that the guard commander had been replaced. He marched into the room, saw the snooker on the TV and shouted that he 'Fucking hates snooker' and that there was a film on the other side, so switched it over. The gutted looks on every other face in the room probably bolstered his flagging ego somewhat, then just to rub salt in the wounds one of us was ordered to make his tea.

I spent the rest of the night on guard trying to find out what had happened. Of course history will recall Dennis Taylor bagged the black that Steve Davis bottled. It wouldn't have made any difference had I witnessed it, but that guard commander, if you are reading this, which I doubt, I'm still holding you to blame.

Basic training came and went with too much trying to get through basic training than punting, and once completed I was sent just up the road to Bordon from Arborfield. Bordon is a small town just outside of Petersfield. The School Of Electrical and Mechanical Engineering, S.E.M.E (everything in the army has an abbreviation) or Prince Phillip Barracks was on the outskirts. There wasn't a lot there but they did have a bookies, a little traditional shop on the hill. It was a real basic one but was just a few minutes' walk from the barracks. The place was small and just one room with a counter at the end of the room and one big table. There was one regular who seemed to live in there. He was the same every day, his Sporting Life was always taken apart and folded so that he could see the selection box for each meeting and each race as the time rolled around. This he studied through a fog of fag smoke and rarely said a word.

My interest in racing hadn't waned in the time I was embarking on 8 mile runs, being barked at by a red-faced corporal, scrubbing toilets and polishing boots. I got the Sporting Life when I could as well as watching the racing where possible. When I got to Borden things were a lot more relaxed than they were back in depot. We were squaddies with inspections and guard duty, but we were effectively students, learning how to fix vehicles taking lessons, practical and theory.

The wages went up too so I spent what was half of a week's wages on the latest edition of the Timeform Chasers and Hurdlers and set about studying it. It was a lovely item, leather bound and glossy paged, containing all the Timeform ratings and the font of all knowledge when it came to beating that bookie down on the hill. The trouble was, I was in a room of four and we were young lads so our evenings heading into The Royal Oak in Petersfield and days trying to learn how to fix a Stalwart amphibious vehicle didn't really lend themselves to serious study. My punting was no more successful than it had been in Tiverton but I was still hooked. I did try to get some of my mates involved, but it didn't take many losing days, to put them off. The final friend who had kept the faith finally called it a day when a treble that we had just got up was snatched from our lips by the faceless stewards.

Despite the fact nobody else was interested I was still adventurous and wanted to spread my racing wings. I decided that I would take a trip to Sandown Park one Saturday. It was a jumps meeting and I made the trip by train. I do remember the incredulous looks as I marched up to the guard room to sign out dressed in my suit and trilby clutching my binoculars. It looked for a minute as if they had assumed I was an officer and sort of stiffened up, then relaxed into smirks when they clocked it was me.

I had never been to Sandown before, not forgetting that up to this point my racecourse experience could be counted on the digits of one hand. I arrived by train, you take a short walk from the platform down some steps and have to walk across the course to the stands. It was an impressive sight, one that became more impressive when I got into the course itself, it was amazing to me. It sounds weird now but one of the things that struck me was the fact that they had escalators and was so big and glamorous.

It was also a lot more rakish in the ring. Of course some of the London bookmakers used to make it to Cheltenham and Chepstow but this was the real deal. My senses were being bombarded by the rich throng of race-going humanity. Guys in calve-length camel coats who must have been gangsters for sure, bookmakers barking prices with a team around them that had to have been mates with the Kray twins, rich people and uptown girls that I could only dream of meeting. The ring was huge and bustling and I soaked it all in. Cheltenham and Chepstow had affected me but this time I was absorbing this all on my own, it was a tale to tell Larry and the rest of the William Hill guys. I was living the dream and actually rubbing shoulders with real professional punters, after all, most of these people had to be didn't they?

One other excellent bit of excitement, John McCririck was in the ring for Channel 4. I hovered around and got his autograph. He was some sort of punting hero to me at the time standing shoulder to shoulder with the punters against those dastardly bookies. I waited to position myself behind him when he went on air. I could only imagine the guys back home when they saw me there. To my mind it was a local boy made good story. It worked, I was on the telly. I didn't know at the time but the next time I was on leave one of the White Horse hooligans told me that he had seen me on TV.

I never saw it myself of course but if this gets published and Channel 4 fancy digging out their archives, I'd love to see it all these years later. The racing itself is a bit vague to me now. I remember backing one winner and promptly going to the Turf Newspapers kiosk to buy the hardback edition of Alex Bird's book 'Life and Secrets of a Professional Punter.' I did most of my money on a hotpot, I got on at 8/11. I have a feeling the horse went off much shorter because I recall 'Big Mac' telling the viewers at home that some 'shrewdies' got on at that price. My chest swelled a bit there. I was on at that price therefore I had just been described as a 'shrewdie' by the face of UK racing television. I stood on the little step just up from the rails in front of the number one pitch and waited to collect my money, the race just needed to be run first. I remember very well looking around me and up to the glass-fronted restaurant and thinking 'This is what I want to do, this is where I want to be', I have read power of suggestion theories, if they are correct that is where the seed was sown in my subconscious.

The hotpot was beaten by a 25/1 shot called That's Your Lot trained by rookie trainer and recently retired champion jockey John Francome. I boarded the train skint but happy and headed back to barracks with my head buried in the life-story of one of the most successful professional punters the country had ever seen, Alex Bird.

Despite having the benefit of gleaning the knowledge of Alex Bird's punting life, the rest of my time at Bordon was spent losing the battle against the bookie on the hill. Newly qualified and the proud recipient of an HGV III license I was posted to Germany. I had a good send-off though. The day before I flew to my new life in the Fatherland I was glued to the TV for the coverage of Cheltenham. Thursday's Gold Cup was one of the races that has gone down in National Hunt folklore. I had backed Forgive N Forget and looked to be on a winner three out but it was all about Dawn Run who forged clear on the run-in to beat Wayward Lad for a famous victory. Just watching on the TV at Larry's place the atmosphere was electric, one of those days where it dawned on me that racing was about much more than winning money. The passion there, even in a living room miles from the course, was palpable.

Army life in Germany was a whole new world compared to the 'bullshit', to coin an Army phrase, at depot and Bordon. We lived in a camp that was made up of ground-level buildings built along corridors that looked like they must have been there since the 1950s. We had a 9 to 5 job working in the workshops fixing the vehicles that the R.C.T. broke. Between our rooms and the workshop we had a N.A.A.F.I.. That place was marvellous and at 10am every morning they had the daily papers in stock and ready to sell. No Sporting Life though. They hadn't even heard of it, but were reassured when I informed the ladies who worked there that it was a daily paper like The Sun, well sort of. I was warned that it would be expensive; they were informed that I didn't mind. Within a week Craftsman Nott was spending his mid-morning breaks reading the Sporting Life and The Weekender on Thursdays.

I was in splendid isolation with my interest in racing though did try to drum up some followers on Saturdays; we only had one channel so the racing was on most weekends. I did organise the odd sweepstake. Occasionally there were more people who wanted to throw a mark into the pot than there were runners, so I used to add a few extra. All Eight Ran was a favourite (insert actual amount of runners) along with a liberal sprinkling of names like Youvedoneyourmoney or Unluckyforsome. Nobody was getting ripped off because they knew the perils and of course there was always a happy winner. I did spend quite a lot of time on the form and did OK betting using my accounts, always making sure that I queued early with plenty of 1 DM coins to call my bookies and to get in front of all the lovelorn squaddies hogging the phone for hours calling home.

One of my gambling mates from Tiverton was also in the Army and lived in a camp an hour or so away. We got together and joined a racing club. MDM Racing (Thoroughbreds) Ltd were based in York and cost about £200 a year. For that you got a monthly photo of one of your horses and a newsletter. There was also a telephone number for news that gave you all the latest info on your horses. They had paid £20,000 guineas for a hurdler called Rockmartin. This beast was destined for great things. The idea was that we were going to stop doing our usual mug bets. At this point I have to assume that my betting wasn't anywhere near as good as I alluded to earlier, and just lump on big when one of ours got the green light. At this point we both had the rather touching faith in the belief that the stables always knew when one of theirs was going to win. So we were going to have it on, wait for the money to roll in and when we had enough buy our own horses, leave the army and continue to do the same bigger and bigger levels and rake it in. No, my eternal optimism never seemed to wane!

Rockmartin was set to make his debut on Boxing Day 1986. We were going to have it spark off. My mate's non-racing brother was posted to the same camp as me so we were all spending Christmas together. It was freezing cold and snowing as we huddled into the yellow phone box just outside of the guardroom to listen to the race. There was no way we could hear the race without help because in those days the commentary lines were all on premium numbers that it wasn't possible to dial from Germany. I called William Hill for our £100 bet, £50 each, which was a nice few quid bearing in mind that we earned about £20 a day each, before tax. I explained our situation to the guy on the phone who agreed to patch us into commentary. Being a Boxing Day it was a very busy day and the commentary darted from one place to another. There was a delay at Wetherby so we hung on and hung on, the huge pile of 1 DM coins were being eaten in an alarming manner, still no race. 'Are you sure you want to hang on?' interjected the voice after we had just listened to trap 6 win somewhere. We were, still more delay. Still the pile deleted, still more delay, no word from Wetherby, more delay, the last coin in the slot, click.

There was no hope of listening to the race now. The only thing for it was to get back to my mate's brother's place and sit glued to the Ceefax and await the result. The delay was a good hour, then finally we were put out of our misery, 2nd, behind a horse of Gordon Richards called High Plains. We were gutted. Eventually the winner proved to be a top class horse but that was hardly any consolation to two heartbroken squaddies who had just had Christmas ruined even had they known at the time.

As explained, the winner went on to be a great horse, but Rockmartin went on to be second, a lot. The rich pot of punting gold didn't turn out as we expected, and what was really brought home to us was the reality of racing. We had a frustrating time. A horse called Senor Ramos never ran well when it was expected to then won at 12/1, care of a steward's enquiry, when it wasn't fancied at all. Some of the horses that were going to be good things never ever looked like winning. We also had some successes though, a horse called Payvashooz was the first two year old to win twice and later on Tyrnippy won at 11/1 when I was on. It was an excellent insight into the reality and unpredictable nature of the real world of racing rather than the predetermined nature of the races, the idea I sort of had prior to that point.

I had to share a room with Geordie Prescott and it is fair to say he was a bit of a messy bugger. His side of the room was in fact all of the room so I had to be a bit insistent that I got mine. He was a nice bloke but had a habit of buying fried chicken and kebabs from the van that used to pull into the camp at around 10pm. He'd then eat it in bed, put the well-sucked bones on the bedside, wipe his hands on his duvet and then drift into slumber.

When my tucker-keen Sunderland fan, he wasn't all bad, roommate was posted the rooms were upgraded and for a while I had my own space. I got some stuff together, luxury big items like sofas and fridges were often up for grabs when people moved on. I didn't fancy taking anything off Geordie though. The swing bin full to the brim with scrunched up toilet paper which was found part-buried by his bed was heaved into a skip wearing rubber gloves.

I was considered to be a bit strange. My love of old rockabilly music and horse racing set me apart from a lot of squaddies, especially when we had the odd room inspection. My framed photos of Rockmartin, Senor Ramos and collection of form books that decorated my bedspace as opposed to Sam Fox and Linda Lusardi were quite stark. I got on with everyone though and had a nice time in Bunde. Another landmark in 1986 was The Racing Post. The Naafi ordered it in for me from the first issue and it soon became my staple diet instead of the Sporting Life but I still got the Weekender and kept the form pull-outs. My mate and I made sure we had leave together and made sure we got some racing in.

One of those occasions I proudly drove my new to me, on credit, bright red, second-hand BMW home. Just as I was about to lord it up driving around Tiverton the purr of the finely-tuned engine suddenly turned into something more akin to what I was used to working with in Germany. The downpipe had blown. Being a left-hand drive I was gutted because the earliest the part could be obtained left a day or two before my leave was over. We had a trip to Salisbury planned, their big meeting of the year sponsored at the time by Veuve Clicquot champagne. There was one thing for it, copious amounts of 'Gun Gum.' It was really only intended for patching up small holes on a temporary basis but three tins later my badly blown downpipe was fixed. We were used to improvising in the R.E.M.E. and I was quite proud of the job.

We drove the hour and a half or so to Salisbury with the BMW purring like it should. It was still cat-like as we were directed into the car park. The car park was, and still is, a field.

The problem was it appeared to have been badly rutted at some point and then dried, so as I was directed to my place at the other side of the field we shook, rattled and rolled then shook a bit more but all seemed well. It wasn't, the whole mould had cracked and mostly fallen off. We had a great time at the races but it took a long time to get home sounding and performing like a tractor.

In 1987 I was sent on tour attached to another unit working in the workshops of a barracks. The RCT guys used to get the papers in every day so I didn't go short on my fix of the Racing Post. We were pretty busy for the four months we were over there but I kept in touch with the racing. There was a guy who looked, acted and talked like an officer, but wasn't. He was keen on racing though knew little. He started asking me to put bets on for him. I started to do so but after a while decided to stick them myself, just before the bugger had a jammy run. He did win a few quid off me to begin with but as his confidence grew he lost it all back to me.

I did have a bit of rather cruel fun with my squaddie mates when Reference Point won the Great Voltigeur at 1-14. I told all my pals he was a certainty and that if they wanted to bet me a pint each if he lost I would buy them all two pints each. To people that didn't really understand racing it seemed a great bet so they jumped in. That Saturday night, at the disco they used to throw for us, I drank for free despite the Derby hero losing a shoe in the race. It was while I was over there that Lester Piggott was jailed for tax evasion. It didn't take too much working out who painted the graffiti 'Free Lester Piggott' on the workshop wall but nobody seemed to mind too much.

We were allowed a weekend of R&R in the middle of our four month tour. I managed to coincide my leave with the weekend that hosted the inaugural 'Festival of British Racing' at Ascot, another track I was hugely impressed with. I have no idea what even ran now, but I do remember not backing a winner. I spent most of my time in the betting ring soaking up the atmosphere, sights and sounds as per usual when I got to go racing.

We used to get a bit of extra money being on tour. This was mainly because we didn't have to pay for our food and lodgings. It was just as well as it was four men, to what was little more than a 'portacabin.' With the money I had got together I was off shopping with one thing in mind, a proper 'Michael Dickinson' coat. It was quite humorous as my mate and I walked into a posh gentleman's outfitters, not the sort of the place young hoodlums, as we appeared to be, would venture into.

When I started pawing a genuine amber coloured Crombie overcoat one of the assistants came over, tape measure around his neck and sniffily asked if he could help but really meaning, 'bugger off there is nothing for you here.' With a bit of youthful bravado I pulled out £200 in tenners and said I'd like to try on the coat. On hearing our English accents and seeing the money the tape-measure clad chap's demeanour changed in an instant. I assume he was under the assumption that we were officers as it wasn't really the clobber your average squaddie would buy. The coat fitted a treat so I swiftly spent about 8 day's wages on it. I was informed that I had been the first 'gentleman' to purchase one of these this season so was given a complimentary zip up bag to go with it. The guys back at the camp could not believe it as I was prancing up and down the corridor catwalk style. They were incredulous that anyone would want to wear such an item. When my mate told them how much I had spent on it, their niggling thoughts that I was a bit mad were confirmed.

Whilst on tour I was ever more keen to get involved in racing. I was also starting to make targets about money I was going to need to get together to get out of the Army. After my tour, even though I wasn't doing anything dangerous, I felt I had done my bit. Going home also heightened my awareness that things were going pretty well back in Civvy Street. My mates back home were earning plenty of money in the building trade, loads more than we got being bossed about and having to work on the whim of people I didn't consider to be better than me, just born with a silver spoon. I spent an afternoon writing letters to clerks of courses asking if they could employ me for a day when I was on leave.

Every one of them said yes, either to a job ( I worked on the 'Owners and Jockeys' entrance at Huntingdon), or sent me free tickets (Newbury for the two days of the Hennessy meeting), all that is except for Nottingham. That was a shame because I was to start my week travelling the turf visiting the yard of John Mackie, the trainer of a couple of our horses. That was an excellent day. There are photos of me in my green wellies and crombie sporting a centre parting (where that came from I don't know, my hair, when not skinned by the army was always a greasy Elvis clone) proudly posing with the horses. I was very grateful to Garry Marshall who sorted it for me as I was never able to go to the organised stable visits.

I didn't have long to settle back into life in Bunde. I was to take part in Exercise 'Med Man' in Canada in the spring. I was very pleased about that and enjoyed the month I was over. I left my mate Larry with the phone number to the MDM racing hotline and some readies telling him to back any of our horses accordingly. There was a horse called Mazercanova that was running so well at home but only officially selling class but had been working with decent horses. 'He only has to turn up to win, the rest need not bother' was the message. Larry backed it with my money accordingly. The horse ran terribly, just one of those horses that didn't put it in on the day, according to the very cheery voice on the end of the line, Garry Marshall.

Exercise Med Man was a live firing event held on the prairies of Alberta which saw us working shifts fixing prop shafts and the like when the trucks used to take ammo and fuel to the gunners and tanks came in for servicing. There wasn't much opportunity to follow the racing whilst the month-long exercise went on but I had done my homework for R&R. The city of Calgary had been in the news the previous months with the epic, brave but slightly foolhardy exploits of Eddie 'The Eagle' Edwards. The snow had been replaced almost overnight by searing heat but Calgary had one main attraction for me, a racecourse, 'Stampede Park' at the Saddle-Dome where the annual Calgary Stampede was also held.

Much to the merriment of my mates I had packed my suit in readiness for the races and persuaded them all that rather than Montana and Las Vegas where a lot of the other squaddies were headed, Calgary was the place to go. One Greyhound bus trip later we were at our weekend's accommodation, the International Hotel that even had a concierge and was only $55 a room per night, for rooms much nicer than the one I had stayed in for double the money on Park Lane when dad won a building award the previous December. There was no time to waste, the racing was on that afternoon, none of my mates could be talked into coming with me when there were bars downstairs so I donned my best suit and asked the concierge to hail me a taxi to Stampede Park.

The racecourse was the first I had visited outside of the UK and was quite strikingly different. The dirt surface for starters and then the entrance fee which was a bargain $4 for the Club enclosure. I stood out like a sore thumb. There I was dressed for Ascot and pretty much everyone else there was dressed as if they had been tending cattle on the ranges, and to be fair a lot of them probably had. One idiosyncratic thing about proceedings at this racecourse steeped in the Wild West was before every race a guy appeared to toot on a hunting horn dressed in full hunting pinks. I wasn't the person who stood out the most after all, not that I minded of course.

There were 10 races all detailed in a king-sized racecard. The meetings there last for days and I had arrived at the tail end of one. The advantage for the punter was that the same horses had been running against each other on the same course mostly over the same distances. I sat down and narrowed down the fields then watched the tote betting (no bookies of course) and backed accordingly. To cut a long story short, the tactic was quite successful, so successful in fact that I settled everyone's hotel bill in cash with my winnings.

I was on a roll so on my return I strode purposefully into a small subterranean casino full of almost exclusively Chinese people and headed for the roulette. I had a new system, all I had to do was identify someone enduring a bad run of luck then oppose them. I watched for a bit and spotted what I was looking for, 'a loser.' There he was having a torrid time, sweating and looking generally flustered. He piled his stack of chips on red so I put my solitary $20 on black, watched the ball land on red then bounce onto black, cashed in my chips and left to find my mates.

The rest of the evening was spent celebrating and is a bit hazy but involved getting into a cab on my own and asking to be taken to a 'hillbilly' bar. Dancing the night away in a club called The Saddlers was like something out of Dukes of Hazzard then having to escape when a lady of (very) advancing years declared that she'd only known me an hour, but was in love with me and that her husband 'didn't treat her like a woman.'

While I was in Canada I decided for certain that I was going to apply to leave the Army via the premature voluntary release procedure. For the princely sum of a month's wages you could buy yourself out after three years completed following basic training. That meant June 1988, I applied and was told that it was a formality and that I had done my bit. My mate in the office told me that all would go through. I was going to be a 'civvy' again before the year was out and could hold my head up high because I only intended to serve three years anyway. My name, rank and number on my door were replaced by S J Nott esq 'Gentleman Of The Turf' and the guys all started to call me Gent.

My next leave was filled with optimism and got me rubbing shoulders, literally with my racing hero. MDM racing had a rare runner in the south; Tyrnippy was entered to run at a Windsor evening meeting. According to the MDM racing hotline with Garry Marshall, Tyrnippy was fancied. I borrowed my mum's little red mini and headed up the motorway to see 'my' horse run and back it accordingly. It was the first time I had ever been to the course and was totally engrossed by it, lovely red brick buildings, a whole host of characters, the garden party atmosphere and the sunshine. Our horse was a 9/2 shot so I marched over to the rails, as owners do, don't you know, and asked the representative of Victor Chandler the price of Tyrnippy. They quoted 9/2 and I proudly quoted my account number, 3301 if I remember rightly and had £20 each way. The rep and his guy looked at me a bit old fashioned, I thought that a bet of a day's wages each way was a fair bet, but to them it was more trouble than it was worth especially on the account.

The racecourse was packed so being short of stature I decided to be professional and find a television on which to watch the race. As they were off I was firstly aware of cigarette smoke and a be-hatted gentleman standing next to me. I glanced over, then did a double take and glanced over again before restoring my cool and composure quickly looking back to the TV before I appeared weird. It was none other than Barney Curley. Soon the race was approaching its business end, my thoughts about Barney were banished for a furlong as Tyrnippy looked to be travelling well, took the race up well inside the distance. My trip to Windsor was going to be a dream, until it was shattered by a horse called Eternal Triangle, almost on the line.

We were second. I glanced down to my racecard, then up quickly and looked across at my non-smiling but very content looking fedora resplendent neighbour open mouthed. There was no way of telling if he had backed it, but I was pretty certain my horse had been done by my hero while he stood next to me, I didn't know whether to laugh or cry, but sort of felt empathy with bookmakers for a few seconds. I accepted that we had been beaten by a better man and due to my cautious each-way staking hadn't lost more than a round of drinks. I drove home humbled but happy leaving before the last.

The rest of my leave was taken up with planning my business empire on leaving the Army. My mate Larry had stopped being a professional punter for some reason and started a carpet cleaning business. I was quite chuffed that he'd asked if I would like to come into partnership with him. So it was all sorted, I started making plans for world carpet cleaning domination and Larry sent me a book, Terry Wogan's 'To Horse To Horse' to read on my way back.

All set to come home in a couple of weeks, out of the blue I was given the, at the time, devastating news that due to small print I was not going to be able to leave until March 1989 because as I had been trained at S.E.M.E., I had to give the army three years after my college training, rather than after basic training. Not only that, the powers that be had decided that I was worth keeping so was to be posted in the hope that a change of scenery would change my mind about giving up an army career.

A few weeks later I was off to another camp. I wasn't very popular there at all. The CO didn't know that I had a PVR (Premature Voluntary Release) active until I arrived and had my 'welcome to the new camp and what are your Army ambitions' meeting so was jolly annoyed when he found out that I was dead wood palmed off on him. I faced the wrath of his revenge for the first few weeks, guard duties and stints painting white lines in the car park at weekends. The latter was speeded up somewhat when the poor other unfortunate who was to suffer the same fate with me and I created a contraption that allowed us to paint neat white lines in one go. We used two pieces of wood to paint between rather than the painstakingly slow way we had been shown. The hierarchy were not too happy but secretly sort of chuffed that we had used our initiative. After all, we were R.E.M.E. and the top 10% of the Army as they had kept telling us in basic training. This of course was, and no doubt still is, true.

Wanting to leave the army was pretty much frowned upon by all ranks so it took me a bit of time to be accepted by my colleagues but I, as they say, screwed the bob in, and got on with my work. One of the turning points was a room inspection. Once again I had put my horse photos on the wall of my bed-space. As it turned out the workshop boss was also into horses and was very impressed that I had fillies and not fannies up on my wall. As time went on he was even more impressed that I had betting accounts and could get on. That was Craftsman Nott off the Saturday guard rota and invited to the boss's house to watch the racing and place bets.

Having been previously warned that my PVR form was going to have to pass through several people's hands and could sit on desks gathering dust it all of a sudden started to fast track. I was presented with nut and bolt man made into a guy sat on a shooting stick next to a winning post looking though some outsized bins at a leaving do at the end of Feb. I was back at Depot in Arborfield signing off and a civilian again bang on the earliest date I was allowed. Racing had helped get my less than illustrious Army career ended without too much pain.

# Chapter 3

*Service to Queen and Country completed – turf time.*

In the interim period of thinking I was going to be out of the army and actually being out of the army, the idea of going into business with Larry was amicably shelved in favour of going it alone as a man and a steam cleaner service. I was promised more work than I could cope with, funnily enough by the guy who had the kit to sell which I could perform at a promised £10 an hour. I jumped at it and quickly got a loan for a second hand van and steam cleaning ensemble. The guy who sold me it promptly got me a job cleaning a milking parlour that paid £45. That might not sound a lot, but I earned it in a day and was more than twice as much as I would have earned in the army. Sadly I didn't get any more at all from him. I was proactive however and knuckled down advertising in the local paper, which didn't yield much work, and racecards at local meetings, that did. Before I knew it I was cleaning huge free-range chicken houses and then started sort of living the dream cleaning the boxes at Exeter and Bath racecourses. I also cleaned ex-jockey Neil Kernick's boxes. This was it, I was on the inside and going places.

Sadly things started to go a bit wrong, my machine packed up and was then 'fixed' with a dodgy part so I got behind with very time-sensitive chicken sheds, losing that work was a near disaster. The loans still needed paying and I hadn't been very good with the money I had earned. Then came the phone call I opened this book with.

I had been racing at the local tracks a fair bit since I had left the army and started 'Superlative Power Cleaning' (older readers will remember Bill O'Gorman's sprinter) and had watched Dave work the floor for Jack Lynn. I was familiar with the ring at the point, at least in the south-west and knew what the job entailed, and of course, tic-tac. I had really fancied working on course so jumped at the chance to get involved. I remember my first day very well. It was a lovely sunny evening so I turned up in what most people would probably describe as a hideous multi-coloured Caribbean style shirt that I had bought in Canada (there were matching three-quarter length shorts to go with it that I couldn't afford because I had spent all of my money in hillbilly clubs and on beer, I was gutted about that). Jack and his son Roy appeared to both recognise me but also seemed a little dubious, but they needed a floorman so weren't going to complain.

It didn't take me long to get into their good books. In those days the market in Tattersalls didn't really get underway until around 10 minutes before each race. Bookies and their staff had a chance to relax before a hectic betting heat that was repeated throughout the afternoon. The later the market was active the more the rush for the punters to get on and the better the margin for the layers.

Most rings had a firm that would generally stick his neck out and price up early. He would do so with a very good margin but still caught a cold on occasion when the punters piled in for one. Of course they were pretty good at what they did so more often than not got horses into the book well under the odds too. In the southwest first up was normally a bookmaker called Eddie Baxter. He was a sturdy bespectacled chap with close cropped snowy hair who traded under the name of 'Avalon' with the legend 'Ave It On With Avalon' on his kit. He was one of the very few books in the ring at that time who would lay bets as small as £2 each way, most were a fiver minimum. Eddie Baxter was betting a few places up from us with his back facing the course and facing the row of books on the other side of the ring. This was and still is quite unusual and gave the bookmakers a good view of each other.

I went to the front of Eddie's joint and wrote the prices of each horse in the box that I had separated the bit of paper into, with the names and numbers that coincided with the horses in the position on the board. There was a short one in the race at 4/5. I read the odds out to Roy in my best bookies' slang doing my best to impress. He priced up accordingly after I had waited for a bit to make sure that Eddie wasn't knocked over by shrewdies. Almost as soon as he priced up Jack was handed a monkey by a lady that they seemed to know. At that point Eddie Baxter removed the 4/5 from his board. Bugger, I thought, now I am in trouble, the price has gone and Jack has been lumbered with a lump of clever money. Just as my heart sank Eddie chalked up the unusual price of 9/10. I rushed over to tell Roy who leapt off his box still clutching his book and sprinted the few places to Avalon and called in a £450 - £500 thus obtaining a bet of £50 to nothing.

He reported what he had done with Jack who allowed himself a big smile that elevated his white handlebar moustache's end skywards. He beckoned me over and said the words that would have been so different had Avalon gone 4/6f. 'Well done boy, you just earned your wages with the first words that came out of your mouth.' There were two other regular guys who worked for the Lynns but after the first bet in the very first race I was on the team.

It was that very first day working on the racecourse that I was to hear a phrase that I have heard over and over again when there had been a crisis in the betting ring. A veteran floorman by the name of John Holland came up to say hello and welcome me to the betting ring, then added that I should enjoy it but I had come in too late because the 'game had gone.' Jack was to christen John 'The Shop Steward' because he always had an opinion and was often saying things to bookies' workmen that made the bookies themselves cringe, things like after such great results there was bound to be a bonus at the end of the day. This was usually aimed at chaps who had the reputation for being a bit stingy when it came to paying their staff. He'd drop the bomb then wander off chuckling to himself.

At the time I still had some work with my steam-cleaning business but was flexible so ideal with the Lynns. The two other guys were always available for local meetings like Exeter, Newton Abbot and Taunton but were either not able or so keen to travel further afield so I was the 'go to' guy for mid-week meetings like Bath, Newbury, Salisbury and Chepstow.

For anyone given the chance to get into the on-course business there could be no better apprenticeship than with the Lynns. The way things were back in those days were that pitches were allocated to bookmakers and although they didn't own them they were theirs to bet in and hand down to their sons. The only way a newcomer could get a pitch was work their way up the waiting list. These waiting lists were sometimes decades old and often very long. They were also quite often disputed with tales of names removed and leap-frogged on lists, missing lists and even tragic fires that destroyed lists. The only way anyone could progress up these lists was in 'dead man's shoes.' A firm had to go to the wall or the pitch-holder die with no heir for people to move up one. There were always suspicions that bookmakers rising the list who were from out of the area, faces didn't fit or deemed too strong were sometimes run rough-shod over but of course none of these rumours really had any substance, especially if the fires or burglaries were thorough!

# Chapter 4

*A racecourse regular for Jack Lynn*

Jack Lynn had worked on course since the 1960s but due to the snail-like pace of the lists, had to bet in unfavourable pitches at the majority of courses. As with the high street, the position of your business had a massive effect on your turnover. To exacerbate the situation every so often bookmakers in bad pitches got to taste the good life when positions became vacant. If meetings clashed there would often be 'move-ups', people from lesser pitches got to shuffle up. There was also a seniority rule which meant that when it came to moving up, bookmakers like Jack who were in relatively poor pitches but had held them for a number of years, leapfrogged firms where the father had died or retired and passed the business on to his son. Such was the advantage to these moves that firms would quite happily up sticks and move all their kit even for the last race. Working in the better pitches meant you took more money and could probably do so at shorter odds with the added advantage that if you did lay one that was a bit too thick you should normally be able to easily hedge the bet in the rows behind, quietly earning from your bet at bigger odds.

There were quite often envious looks from the back row to their brethren paying the same expenses in the better pitches but that was how it was and you just got on with it. So the apprenticeship was extra difficult because the Lynns were bookmakers in the traditional sense of the word. Jack's son Roy was fantastic with figures, he could tell at a glance if they, the figures, were good or bad for the ring so knew when to get to work or to hang fire. Some layers were form experts that burned the midnight oil and had a plan for the day's racing. They would tread water for a few races then bet to their opinion when they thought they could get a short one beaten. Others would just take what the punters threw at them but the Lynns bet to figures. They would have the favourite a loser in the race quite often but the value had to be there. They weren't in the game of taking huge bets but would do if they thought they could hedge it and earn, within reason of course. Punters who wanted huge bets generally knew where to go. Being in the back row the margins we had to bet to were thin so the floorman (me) had to be totally on the ball because if you went to sleep and missed a price going there was very little option for hedging. It is fair to say that if the Lynns laid 7/1 and you only got 13/2 back you would not be flavour of the month.

Working on the floor meant that you had to bristle with your senses all at work for price movements. You'd spot the bookmakers all removing the same price in quick unison, the 'knockover' was a bit like a snowball so you should spot it. The art of being on the floor was spotting the more subtle market moves. A known big punter going into one of the ring's bigger layers, that bookie discreetly removing that price and sending his floorman scampering off would possibly be a prelude to a move. Those sorts of things take a while to learn so I was lucky that despite a few fortunately not too costly early mistakes, the Lynns were happy to use me.

One of the first things a floorman needed to learn were fractions. Bookmakers back then, and to a certain extent even now, would lay the fractions. These prices were a throwback to the days when odds were in the '100 to' format. When the prices were simplified 100/14 became 7/1 which trimmed a bit of value from the punters though if someone wanted to back a horse to win £100 and it was 7/1 a layer would generally bet a punter, mainly because it was a lot easier for the clerk to write in the field book ledger.

41

Bookmakers would always (with just the odd one or two exceptions) lay each other fraction bets so if you did get lumbered with a bet at 7/1 that you didn't really want all of or that was sticking out in your book, you could send the floorman off to get a bet back at 100/14 so earning yourself a bit. I had to learn these fractions, they ranged from 11/2 (100-18) to 66/1 (200-3). What made things more difficult was that I would rarely be sent off to have a £1000 to anything, we bet to much smaller figures so it would be more often than not an order to back a horse to win £250 best you can do. It may not sound like difficult maths but you needed to get the bet right because if you couldn't work it out under pressure, you would be often made to look like an idiot if you asked one of the busier layers for your bet and you couldn't call in £250 - £35. Some of the bigger egos seemed to revel in taking the mickey, especially should you be asking for a bet at the lower end of the scale.

Although floormen were the eyes and ears of the bookmakers they weren't necessarily held in high esteem with the layers, not Jack anyway. One afternoon at a desolate rain-swept midweek meeting a bookie looked up to Jack and then around to the overpopulated by bookmakers betting ring and said, 'It won't be a lot of good here Jack, there're no punters.' Jack replied, 'Oh I don't know, there are plenty of floormen who will have a bet and they are all c**nts', never one to mince his words.

It was to be said that the Lynns were hard to work for but perfect for getting good at what you do quickly. My name soon became known around the racecourses. If I couldn't be seen the moment a bet was laid it was screamed out, and often repeated by mickey taking layers around us. That wasn't a bad thing because the patronising side came in handy 'helping the boy out' so I could pretty much always get a back bet on even if it was gone.

Some others took the opposing view and came out with

comments like 'I'll lay you what he'd lay me
were at least better than the 'bluffers.' You'd
wait for confirmation, the worst offenders
foot over your head while you waited, rub u.
feign total shock when you asked if you had got th

That was the disadvantageous side but one
advantages of being on the floor and getting on was that ,
didn't have to pay when you called the bets in but settled up
afterwards. That was generally very handy especially when it
was busy and the part of the job I enjoyed the most, dodging
around the ring getting on for the boss. With the Lynns there
was lots of getting on to do.

It wasn't all plain-sailing especially in the very early
days. In fact on my second day I was asked to work we went to
Bath. Bath was a little more daunting. It was the first time I had
been there racing, although I did clean the stables when steam
cleaning. For some reason nobody wanted the front end pitch
so the Lynns got there in the move up. I was told to be lively
because they might get landed with some lumpy bets. Not long
after the betting started for the first race I was screamed for. I
was told to get a bet back on a certain horse. There were two
very close in the betting, I rushed down to the bookmaker Roy
directed me to, stopped in front of his joint and then froze.

I had forgotten the name of the horse and stood there
like a rabbit trapped in the headlights. The bookmaker glared at
me for what seemed like an age, then Roy appeared at my
shoulder still holding his field book and called the bet into John
Tovey. I was told not to worry but was shaken for the rest of the
day, though the glare I caught from the corner of my eye told
me the real story.

Still on the firm, I was unofficially third man and got to
go racing on a fairly regular basis though the existing guys got
to go to the local meetings and prestigious ones like
Cheltenham, at least for a while. I hit it off with Jack pretty

n straight away. He was an eccentric alright but I always avitated to such people, not too strange, after all I had been abelled one in the army. Jack wore a very distinctive handlebar style moustache and was a veteran of the D Day landings, 'Not the first wave though, fuck that' he hastily pointed out. He very rarely talked about his army days but did let on that he suffered from tinnitus ever since being a bit too close for comfort to an exploding mortar shell. Occasionally over-officious car-park attendants got the sharp end of his tongue. He referred to them as corporals, and lambasted them with the occasional, 'The SS scared me but you bloody well don't' followed by a withering stare that would have probably shaken the odd SS man up a bit to be fair.

Jack made no secret of the fact that times hadn't always been as good for him as they were now. He was after all, the richest man in the, albeit fairly small, village. Back in the1960s when betting shops were legalised the on-course market was hit very badly, the waiting lists were not needed then he told me. He confided that nobody has to look skint even if they are and that it was always a good idea to appear affluent especially in the bookmaking game. To that end he let me into a little secret. Quite often back when things were so tough he'd have a job scraping up the tank money to bet with, but of course he didn't want the punters to worry that he may not be able to pay so he used to wrap the few notes that he did have around a portion of toilet roll. When it came to paying out he'd get his 'wad' out from his trouser pocket and peel off the money required. Of course there would have never been a problem paying because Jack ran a tight book out of necessity. It was a strategy that sees him still betting in the ring when flasher types have come and gone in their droves.

Another story he told of his skint days was when he turned up to bet at a point to point at Bratton Down near Tiverton. Only four bookmakers arrived so they had to pay the betting fee pre-agreed with the hunt between just them. This took Jack by financial surprise, he had expected more like a dozen to share the expense. This left him with very little money to bet with so in desperation he bought 'The Pointer' a point to point ratings and tipping guide. He decided to go for the top rated in each race, in other words duck it totally and have it winning him the sum of what he had taken on the other horses. This particular day the guide came up trumps and went through the card. Jack was so flush when he left he was able to upgrade his car on the way home from the races.

Being able to pay wasn't always the way though. Jack told a great story about another bookmaking firm who were betting up on Trundle Hill at Goodwood, way back in the mists of time. A tactic employed by some of the more dubious members of the bookmaking fraternity was to pay out the last race with money you have taken on the next. The idea being that sooner or later a result would come to their aid. This was a very high risk business fraught with danger especially considering places like Trundle Hill were largely un-policed.

On this particular day the results had not gone the way of the bookies. When the last favourite won there was no money left to take and none to pay the winning punters. As the bookmaker tried to hold up payment for as long as possible while they worked out what to do and his partner frantically asked his fellow layers to lend them some money a large hostile crowd was gathering. There was no money forthcoming from others bookies, they had lost badly too, besides the firm's dubious nature was well-known. The crowd started to jostle and things started to look a little dangerous when a member of the firm spotted a dog-collared member of the clergy. He hopped off his box and begged the man of the cloth to intervene. With a performance that was said to have been worthy of the stage he explained how someone had dipped their hod and made off with the entire tank. The firm were mortified that they couldn't pay the winning punters, were desperate to but that they wouldn't listen.

A few minutes later the crowd listened intently as the vicar explained that the poor gentlemen they were threatening had in fact been victims of a heinous crime. As the bookies packed up their gear and all the field money from the last race and hurried to their car the priest was busily collecting names and addresses to where a cheque would be sent in the next post. Quite what his reaction was when he had completed his task only to find the bookies long gone is anyone's guess.

There was none of that sort of skulduggery going on where I was working, though one of my bookie mates did get 'framed' as John Batten the bogus bookie who did a runner from Epsom Downs on Derby day, but more of that later.

At first Jack was a confusing boss to work for. I was told at the start that I wasn't to go near the hod and the money until they knew they could trust me. I didn't take offence at this, in fact I was quite pleased that as I wasn't anywhere near the money I couldn't be the fall guy should any go missing. My peace of mind didn't last long because I was soon trusted to pay out and tidy the cash, but there was one exception, though I wasn't sure if it was Jack's little joke. I was told that I had progressed to being able to delve into the hod but on one condition, I rolled my sleeves up. I no doubt looked a bit quizzical so was given the explanation that back in the mists of time a floorman was caught with elastic bands on his arms up his sleeves. If they were loose enough and the hod was full of readies and he plunged his arms in deep enough he'd 'fish' some notes without anyone being the wiser. If a man was new there would always be a beady eye on him but money up the sleeve was apparently the way to go. To be fair though the bloke had to be a bit thick because if money continues to go missing it won't take long for the perpetrator to be caught and that will be the end of that. Honesty was the biggest qualification for a regular job on the racecourse.

One bookmaker had a little test for new staff. He'd leave a tenner in the hod when setting up before racing. The new guy would be tasked to tidy the hod, get the change ready etc. He'd soon find the tenner. If he handed it to the boss he'd pass, stick it in his pocket and nothing would be said but he'd be forever wondering what he had done never to be asked again.

The vast majority of floormen were totally honest and wouldn't dream of stealing from their boss but some considered earning from back bets to be a grey area. For example, if the boss called his man in and asked him to have a £300 - £100 back and he managed to get £350- £100 some thought that the extra was theirs. He'd report that he'd had what they had asked for then if the horse won trouser the £50. Some layers took this practise more seriously than others. For some it was a sacking offence and seen as stealing while others cast a blind eye, especially if the man was a good workman, though his reputation was always tainted. The practise was always fraught with danger too. Bookies talk so if you had the bet with someone everyone was familiar with, it could always crop up in conversation that their late back bet of £350 - £100 had ruined his book. On the other hand should the bet have been had with a bookmaker from a different area and you weren't known to him it is quite possible he will send his man to confirm that you asked for a £350- £100 back with him. It wasn't unknown for bogus floormen to call in bets, especially at busy meetings.

I saw this in action and was advised by old-sweats that it was all part of the game and your unspoken bonus. I was never of that opinion and thought it was all slightly underhand and considered that if I could prove my worth by beating the price as often as I could it would enhance my reputation and ensure more work. It took me a while to get used to the fractions but I made a point of learning them but always took the precaution of writing them on my racecard in preparation for that

'SIMON!' moment.

Jack and Roy were quite impressed that I knew tic-tac so decided to utilise that skill. Depending on the course we were betting at I would position myself a little further away from the pitch than most floormen.  So not to complicate things I'd just show the prices in racecard order then when a price changed I'd gesture into the general position of the horse on the board then the price and Jack would react accordingly.  If there was a panic station then I'd rush in and take a price straight off the board.  I was quite proud to be trusted with that honour.  Some tactics worked better than others.

One meeting at Chepstow it was decided that I would position myself in the stands.  The drawback from that was that once I was there I was pretty much stuck and unable to get down for any back-bets or rubbing prices off.  The idea was that if they laid a bet that needed hedging I would direct Roy to where the price was available.  It sounded like a great idea but as soon as the first occasion arose to put it into action the scene was quite comical, at least for those around. Roy jumped red-faced and slightly frothing at the mouth, which was how he was when under pressure, and looked up at me wild-eyed making an over the top gesticulation as if to scream 'Where?' I kept pointing to the area where plenty of bookmakers were offering the price he was after, but the more frantically he ran the colder he got.  By the time he realised where I was trying to send him all the prices had gone. I'm not sure if that wasn't because the other books had twigged and just shortened the horse out of devilment.

People liked to take the mick but we were a very professional team who had to keep a step ahead to survive. A fair few of the plans failed but the ones that didn't worked very well. One place where the tic-tac came into its own was at Exeter. Back in those days the ring was set up like a horseshoe. I would stand on three boxes in the middle of the ring and watch all around me and didn't miss much. One afternoon I was filmed by a company that used cameo clips of 'Westcountry Life' on the TV station of the same name. One was just me, entitled 'Tic-tac Simon – Exeter' and the other a wider view of Exeter races featuring several characters from the ring. They were aired on a regular basis during the mid-1990s. They had quite an effect on the oft-stoned hippy that lived in the flat below me when he first saw one, several spliffs in, at 3am. I haven't seen them since but hope they survive and resurface on the Internet sometime along with the clips that are already there.

Sometimes things did get a bit much. Roy Lynn is in my opinion one of the best ever bookmakers in the truest sense of the word but due to the pressure would very often go over the top. One of the things that used to bug me was screaming 'SIMON!' and then ordering me to do something I was already doing or something I considered daft. One day I made a point of proving it. At that time Martin Pipe was sweeping aside the National Hunt world with his innovative training methods that left the old guard toiling in his wake. Martin's father Dave was one of the longest-standing bookies in the ring but you wouldn't get any clues from him but the yard had faces who were worth following. In this case literally, I had noticed Chester Barnes, the Pipes' flamboyant ex-table tennis champion in the ring and was keeping a close eye on if he went in for a bet. Then all of a sudden 'SIMON!' so in I rushed only to be flecked with froth as I was directed to 'Follow Chester Barnes.'

For whatever reason I don't remember but this particularly niggled me. Luckily Chester himself gave me the perfect opportunity to make my point. He wandered down the line of books showing some interest but more than likely just enjoying the buzz he was creating, then headed into the bar area. 'Follow Chester Barnes' had been my order and who was I to argue so follow him I did, through the bar and into the gents and tried not to look too weird as I followed him in. The race was off by the time I got back to the joint. By this time Jack was giving me his steely stare and Roy fit to explode his face the colour of a Swan Vesta match, demanding to know where the (add profanities of choice here) I had been. I couldn't be sure but even Jack allowed himself a smile when I pointed out that Chester Barnes had gone for a pee, then added that I was just glad it wasn't anything more.

My career with the Lynns nearly came to an end one afternoon at Exeter. The meeting had been ticking along quite nicely until the penultimate. The race in question was a tricky looking seller betting about 4/1 the field giving nobody any undue concern other than that you had to keep your wits about you in sellers. Then one of the best executed gambles I had ever seen sprang into action. Bootscraper was bobbing around the 9/2 mark with 5/1 in places. I noticed a guy go into the Lynns and was a bit surprised to see Roy take his 9/2 off the board next to Bootscraper because there was a good bit of 5/1 available with 9/2 either side of them including Dave Pipe, who would lay a decent bet. I was called in and told that they had laid £900-£200 which was a chunk for them and to get £100 back. I told them not to worry I'd get 5/1 then stood in what can only be described as a maelstrom of bookmakers' floormen running around in a panic. To my horror virtually every book had the price next to Bootscraper missing or very short indeed. There was nowhere to go, the horse had collapsed, any price that was reinstated was smashed with the last noted bet laid on the course £600-£400.

There was nothing to do but try and get stuck into the rest of the field but at the off the book had Bootscraper losing a monkey which was a colossal amount the way the firm used to play. I was mortified while Roy paced his way around the ring muttering unmentionable things about me no doubt. Being mortified turned to horror as the gamble went further and further away to win easily. I heard my name and the phrase 'never work for us again' mentioned. I wanted the ground to open up and swallow me and remember almost quitting there on the spot and hitchhiking home. 'The Shop Steward' helped ease the tension that he could see building. He wandered over and started talking in telephone numbers how much people had lost reporting that Stephen Little had been asked for an £18,000 - £4000.

Every bookie he mentioned had lost a lot more than the Lynns. It transpired that the perpetrators of the coup had a man in the ring for every bookmaker. Each had a rough idea how much he could ask each layer for and went in for that amount and did so in a synchronised way. Nobody had gotten away with it. Tales of the fortunes lost seemed to mellow Jack and Roy who soon realised that it hadn't been incompetence on my part but a well-planned coup that tucked the whole ring up. One footnote to the story is that it could have been so much worse. Planners of the gamble must have been dismayed when they opened their Sporting Life that morning to see that, for some unfathomable reason Man On The Spot had napped the horse in his column. Had he not the horse could easily have been a double figures when the gang struck.

Our travelling to and from racing was always quite humorous though not sure it was quite so much fun for poor old Jack as Roy and I used to smoke like trains in the old days. The trips often had a predictable nature because they had their ways. To say Roy and Jack were cautious would be a rather large understatement. It would start the night before racing. Jack would give me a call and tell me a time that I had to repeat back to him, but if there were more than one meeting that we could go to, a clash, he would refuse to tell me where we were going. It was a big thing back when you had to bet in your allocated pitch and good move ups would depend heavily on guessing who would go where. There were various reasons for not telling me. In the early days it was that I might have a drink that night and tell someone who would know a friend of a friend who would tell the other bookies or later on when I was a trustee that the phone might be tapped, by shady bookies no doubt.

The pet hate on summer journeys were caravans. Jack always made me laugh, they were in his words 'Skint mob, a menace that should stay at home in their council houses if they couldn't afford to go on holidays and stay in a hotel.' To be fair the hours we wasted on motorways held up in queues of traffic were nobody's business. The mood would sometimes be lifted as we filed past a stricken caravan with its contents spewed across the motorway but only if the inhabitants of the car were seen safe and well, one less menace on the roads. There were other little routines that had to be gone through. When we went to Newbury we would always take the Hungerford turn off, Roy would start asking us to remind him around the Bath junction and keep doing so. When reminded he'd still feign surprise and repeat 'Is this it?' as we approached our exit. It always made me chuckle or groan depending on my mood.

I used to enjoy going to Newbury. In the days before the new stand it had a lot of character, loads of little nooks and crannies. The bars were old and oozed atmosphere. Good for us poor workers there was a canteen under the stand where you could get some decent food and a drink for a couple of quid. I assume it was for stable staff and racecourse workers but it was full of floormen and clerks too, though the bookies themselves didn't seem to use it. The ring was vibrant and lively full of the sorts of people who I hoped and expected to see in betting rings. There was always someone there selling stuff, jewellery and perfume sometimes but quite often nice suits and camel coats. There was no suspicion to see a rather dapper looking chap marching into the gents being followed by a furtive looking couple of bookies and their better-off staff. There were plenty of people walking around Newbury looking a million dollars though the look had no doubt come at a knock down price, no questions asked.

The over-dramatisation wasn't confined to car journeys though it did manifest itself on the way to my first Cheltenham Festival. The biggest meeting in the UK hadn't featured in the Lynn's year too heavily as they had a poor pitch in Tattersalls but that had all changed a year before. A new 'Lower-Tatts' area had been opened to service the Guinness Village. The Lynns had been persuaded to give it a go. It was a gamble because they had taken years to get on the list for the festival. If the new area proved to be useless there would be no going back. As it turned out, the new area proved to be a goldmine. The pitches were the other side of the Guinness Village with entrances via bars all the way down. At busiest time the punters would stream through to the bookies and almost literally fight to get on.

The books where we stood had no need to keep tugging on the prices as their brethren up in the main ring did, just shorten them as they laid them. The potential was there to make proper books that were rarely seen. The year before all those present had realised what they had dropped into so were keen to get there in plenty of time so as not to miss out on another bonanza. The Lynns being the Lynns we left a good half an hour before even the most cautious of other layers and were in Cheltenham and less than a mile from the course by about 10am. The team that day was Roy, Jack, John the postman and myself. John was first man on the team but occasionally worked for the Jack Bevan firm. When he did so he was envied as they were one of three big firms in the West Country and paid handsomely. They bet in the number three pitch in the main ring and had been a family firm since the late 1800s.

John and I were sat in the back of the car when we hit a small queue of vehicles stopped at a traffic light. Roy suddenly did that head moving thing he did when approaching Swindon after saying don't let me pass Hungerford even though it wouldn't be the end of the world anyway because Newbury was the next turn off. He said something along the lines of 'Oh my God, there's a snarl-up. We're going to be pushed. Dad you may have to get out and start walking now', with that he looked around at John and asked if he thought Dad would make it. John rolled his eyes, let out an expletive and informed Roy that even if we had just found out that we'd left Dad stood on the side of the road back in Somerset, had to wait for the lights to turn green, turn the car around, head back down the M5, pick him up, return and then drop him in the same spot, he'd still be able to walk it. Roy thought for a second and gave a little grin, the lights turned green and within 10 minutes we were in the car park of the still not open Cheltenham racecourse.

As became the tradition for the next few years, annually on the opening Tuesday the place 'Looked a bit thin', probably because we were there so early. The first race was always a little slow, mainly because punters were exploring the course and probably having a drink before they realised it was getting time for the first. 'It's useless' were the phrases coming not just from the Lynns but all over as they fielded money they could not even dream of at any other meeting in the opener. At the off, much to Roy's horror, they hadn't bet 'overs', the first and second favourites were losers in the book. At the line one of them had won. Roy stood with his mouth open, slightly frothing, his hand on his head, and uttered the words 'Johnny Boy, I have to tell you, Cheltenham is over.' John rolled his eyes and handed me the book, so I got started paying out a huge queue of punters while he got started on taking bets for the next race.

The next race was a fair bit busier than the first, in fact it was very busy indeed, so busy that John was as Roy used to say, 'under the cosh.' It would be a good idea to give an idea how the bets used to be recorded before computers took over later in the 1990s. The field-book was a large hardbound ledger. The horses' names would be written one above each column, either in estimated betting order, alphabetical or later on, number order. As the punter approached the bookmaker he'd call the bet, for example, £20 win Carvill's Hill. The bookmaker would then call the bet, for simplicity sake if the horse was 5/4 the bet would be called 'Carvill's Hill £25-20 ticket 123.

The tickets were made of card and stamped individually with a number from 001 to 999, a unique code word and the bookie's name. The clerk would write the bet under the name of the horse with the bet, and in the last column write the total 'takeout' for the horse. If that had been the first bet then the takeout would have been £45. Finally the field money would be, usually scribbled, at the right hand side of the book. The most important figures to get right were the take-outs. A general rule of thumb was that if the bookmaker knew that they were betting to good figures, as long as the take-outs were together then he had a good book, even if the clerk had no idea what the takings were.

As you can imagine the clerk could find himself under immense pressure at meetings like Cheltenham. In the case of John both Roy and Jack were hurling bets at him one after the other. John was lightning-quick but it would be virtually impossible to keep up with everything apart from the most important task, getting the bets down. Things were getting fraught as the time ticked closer to the off of the next. Punters were fighting to get on, Roy and Jack kept calling the bets into John who had his by now sweating head into the book scribbling the wagers down for all he was worth. Roy knew that they must be betting well because he knew the margin they started at was pretty good and he was shortening the prices as he laid them but John had no idea. He was doing his bit shouting 'take that one out' when a horse's column was getting too long, or 'give that a tug' when money was a bit light on one.

At the off, John was the picture of a stressed man. Jack and Roy (with enough froth to tell how busy it had been) wanted to know where they were. Of course none of this barracking was making John's task of pulling out the figures any easier, and he was telling them, in no uncertain terms, to shut the fuck up as he frantically scribbled and did mental calculations. As the horses jumped the last and hurtled up the hill to the line he was still struggling. As the winner was announced it became apparent that there had been a turn-up for the books, to coin a phrase. Roy could see that the column under the name of the winning horse was about an inch long, 'How was it John?' he spluttered breathlessly spitting froth on the figures of the favourite. Exasperated, John put down the pencil not finished but finished as far as the important figures went, looked up through a fringe wet with sweat and replied through gritted teeth, 'Just put it this way Roy, Cheltenham is back on'

The Cheltenham Festival was and still is the most electric meeting in the country, maybe even the world. The atmosphere, the racing, the whole buzz, the craic about the place is totally on its own. Bookmakers in fairly good pitches could bet 'overs' virtually every race back in those days and it was a case of how much were they going to win. Some layers would take a different view and choose to take colossal bets and hope that they got some results that went their way. They could be expected too with the racing being fiercely competitive. But with the Lynns and a lot of the other layers betting the public down in lower Tatts it was more a case of how to field the money, record the bets accurately get the punters paid out and get betting on the next quickly and efficiently.

One of the drawbacks of just trying to get as much money in the hod as possible was that there were plenty of forgeries floating about. At a normal meeting they would stick out like a sore thumb because you handled so much money that a good bag man could tell just by touch or easily spot a dud note. At the festival it was different, notes coming in thick and fast you simply had no time to check each bundle of tens or twenties, if you spotted a moody one it was best just to ignore it and hope it was the only one in the £100 which was more often the case. Picking the notes out and confronting the person trying to pass them would cost more money with the resulting shemozzle in lost bets not taken than taking issue so they were just thrown in the bag; business was that good for a few years not to be an issue. At the end of the day there would be a good sort out of the cash, with a few raised eyebrows when a couple of the notes were virtually no more than photocopies but hopefully no more than a couple hundred quid's worth.

The Lynn's were always ahead of the game. Their problem was getting the bets down. Even John's considerable skills at clerking were pushed to the limit with the volume that was coming into him. It was the best he could do just to record the bets let alone keep the columns up to date. Trying to bet tight and to figures was very important, one miscalculation could prove catastrophic. True to form the next year they had a plan, two clerks. One would write the bets, the other would pull out the take-outs, one book for each race would mean that one of them would pay out at the end of the race while the other started taking bets in the early skirmishes then jump in and help out once things got a bit hectic. The advantages were twofold, betting earlier meant fielding more money and using one of the clerks to pay out meant he was familiar with the bets and betting and would know pretty well when someone was trying it on. The tactic was a good one and stood them in good stead for a couple of years.

The main courses we bet at were the local trio, Exeter, Newton Abbot, Taunton, then further afield at Bath, Chepstow,

Newbury, Salisbury then Cheltenham, Ascot and Goodwood for the big meetings. The local three were where I always felt most at home and soon got to know most of the bookmakers. The 'big three' in respect of time served were Dave Pipe, father of champion trainer Martin. Harry Metcalfe who bet as Jack Bevan, and Bernard Redfern the father of Anthea who older readers might remember from The Generation Game who went on to marry Bruce Forsyth. All eyes were on Dave Pipe's joint when his son had a runner but you wouldn't get a clue from there. Dave just stood there with a deadpan look on his face and generally be market price giving nothing away. It appeared that the staff knew nothing, in fact his next door neighbour on most occasions, Harry Metcalfe used to say that if the staff backed one it was time to get it in the book. There was often a bit of ribbing going on between the pair, more friendly rivalry than animosity, though sometimes things got a bit tense, especially when things had appeared to go horribly wrong.

Harry Metcalfe was an impressive figure well over six feet tall and always immaculately turned out with a crown of silver hair. He'd take on all-comers in a polite manner rarely getting flustered. He'd also let punters bet him in running. Those that fight to get on at 1.03 before a horse has jumped the last hurdle when clear these days wouldn't believe the value. Should an outsider look certain to win he'd quite happily give away a couple of hundred quid in running just in case the horse fell. He'd call even money, (yes you read right) and lay the first comers as they ran in. Pointing to each one that was on, they were told to stay there and wait for their winnings. Should the horse win he'd happily pay, the punters feeling that they had just found money on the floor (which the value they were getting they pretty much had), if it lost he'd take the money from them with a condolence for each one. The fact that every so often a horse did get beaten when it looked certain to win kept that value coming for a long time.

Unlike most West Country bookmakers Harry Metcalfe bet in some prominent positions away from our comfort zone. The front row at Ascot, Cheltenham and Newbury held no fears for him, having worked his way up the waiting list and having been mentored by father Percy. Harry's eyesight started to go a bit at the end of his career; one incident involved his love of laying a rag in front to tidy the book up and a slightly less than scrupulous stand-in clerk. Harry could hear that the horse in front was going well and had glanced down at his book to see that it got him a nice few quid. He had his bins but couldn't really see well enough to ascertain just how well it was going or how far ahead. Harry looked down to his clerk and asked him what price he made the one in front. 'Oh he's a 3/1 shot from there he replied' with which Harry called out '3/1 the one in front', to which the clerk was the first to call in a bet of three score. I can't remember if the horse won or not, but I'd like to think it didn't.

As I cast my mind's eye back round Exeter there is a character on almost every pitch.

Bernard Redfern was the senior bookmaker in the ring by age but braved all weathers to bet in his pitches up and down the country right up until his death. He had an excellent right-hand-man in the shape of 'Bristol' Dave who drove a taxi when not being driven mad by Bernard. He had a very dry sense of humour often wandering over to relate a story or admit that he feared the worse. On one particular occasion Bernard had written 'Get favourite' above a race. Dave had already 'feared the worst' about it, the horse in question had a Gaelic name that could easily be mispronounced, and mispronounced it was by Bernard. Knowing him very well Dave knew which horse he meant as he called bets on the horse relentlessly and got all the wagers down. All the while his omnipresent cigarette burned down to the filter in his lips, the ash dropping on the book.

At the off, Bernard had stood the horse for his maximum which was a fair bit because when he wanted to get the favourite, he got it. Once the race was underway the favourite pronounced correctly by the commentator who was apparently well-versed in Gaelic, certainly better than Bernard, was always going well and never looked like getting beaten. Dave pushed his trilby back over his head and wiped his brow in readiness for a huge pay-out and a grumpy Bernard. 'Told you we'd get that one beat' said a grinning Bernard, before adding 'The commentator never mentioned it once.'

I never had an awful lot of interaction with him but Bernard did make an impression on me. We were betting on a particularly filthy day at Cheltenham. The wind was howling around the ring, the rain was icy and Jack kept sending me to weirder and weirder places to try and monitor the ring and tic-tac from. At the time I was the proud owner of a tan coloured trilby that I hoped made me look like Barney Curley, but by the fourth race the hat was hanging down like the one donned by Ermintrude from The Magic Roundabout. I was cold, wet, miserable and looking forward to going home. Totally out of the blue, or should I say grey, I was tapped on the arm by Bernard who looked colder, bluer and wetter than me with a pendulous dew-drop hanging from his nose, 'Don't start feeling sorry for yourself' he scolded before adding as he spun on his heel, 'You wanted to get into the game.'

Tony 'Conky' Woods was another character; he was from the Yeovil area and wasn't afraid to say things just as he saw them but had a wicked sense of humour and probably the oldest team in the ring. He'd think nothing of wandering up to a very busy bookmaker in full flow, halting his business just to call him an expletive of Anglo-Saxon origin for no particular reason.

By far the biggest bookmaker in Exeter betting ring was Stephen Little, 'the man of mystery' as Jack Lynn called him.

Old-timers remembered the vicar's son cycling to tracks to work on the floor for bookies back in the day. By this time he'd turn up at places like Exeter and Taunton in his Bentley dressed in his mink coat and take on all-comers. It used to be an eye, or rather ear opener, to listen as he called bets in to John his clerk. He would take a £1 each-way followed by a £2000 bet then field a phone call to a take a bet on an away meeting, sometimes very sizeable with apparently no idea of the price of the horse he just laid. Customers knew where to find him if they wanted a big bet. In those pre-exchange days there could possibly have been touches lined up at the tracks he bet at just because he was there, so he had to be careful as the Bootscraper episode proved. If Stephen's team of floormen started to back a horse back it usually meant that the bet was lumpy and from a source he respected. Those guys were the envy of the rest of the workmen in the ring. They always had plenty of money as Stephen was reputed to pay accordingly to his business plus we all assumed that they were privy to the liveliest of information.

Stephen was in his element at meetings like Royal Ascot where he would take on the high-rollers. I'm told he once took a full-page advert out in the Sporting Life with the headline that read something like 'Bet with the little man.' It is said that shortly after he was offered two bets of £90,000 at 4/9, one lost the other won. One bookmaker who was friendly with Stephen but not in the same league when it came to taking bets recalled a day when he was helping him out at Royal Ascot. Little had laid a horse to lose too much even by his own standards. He asked his friend to go and back the horse to win £20,000. He had a task on his hands, the horse had been well-backed all around the ring so a lot of layers were full up with the horse. He managed to back it to win a fraction of what he'd asked for, then as they were off backed it to win another grand calling the bet in to a layer just down the rails.

Legend has it that Stephen was impassive as the horse

won the race with some ease. He sipped on his Diet Coke and asked his clerk what the damage was. Ashen-faced he replied that it was worse than they had thought, he had lost £99,000. With that, the bookmaker who had called in the late hedge bet piped up with apparent sympathy with an 'Oh Stephen, that is a bloody bad bit of luck', Little looked up with a resigned look of gratitude, which soon turned to thunder when his friend added, 'If I hadn't had that last bet it would have been a nice round £100k!'

Not all the 'characters' that lurked in the ring were bookmakers. The staff and punters were a colourful lot too. One much-loved floorman who still attends to this day didn't miss a trick and quite often stuck his neck out to get a few quid. Badger's earning potential started before racing even got under way. He had amassed a huge collection of badges for the local meetings of Newton Abbot and Exeter. They used different colours for each meeting but if you had enough badges like Badger did and took your prized collection with you every time you went it was quite easy to match a previously used badge and get it punched by one of the gatemen.

It was the punching bit that was the problem. Badger was pretty deft at covering one hole with his thumb as he offered his badge over but had to become pretty dextrous when his badge collection started to become a little too perforated. For that reason he could always be seen looking around on the floor for potential additions to his bootie. Once inside Badger's earning potential increased further especially when radios began to be used. He was very proud that on many occasions he worked for two bookmakers at the same time. One based in the Silver Ring who had given him a radio for hedging purposes and the other in Tattersalls. This situation did cause our hero some hairy moments which of course everyone else enjoyed. Badger running around trying to get a hedge bet on feigning technical problems with his transmitting device, despite the fact the whole ring could hear his boss's disembodied voice screaming at him through it.

Not only was Badger adept enough to work for two bookies at once (his claim that he once worked for three was always treated with some scepticism) but he could spot a dropped bank note from the furlong pole. It is said that a note rarely had the chance to even hit the floor before he had grabbed it. One or two bookies said that he spent so much time looking for a scoop he never spotted a price change. His love of a scoop was the subject of some gentle ribbing from other floormen from time to time. One particular occasion he let on to a couple of us his tactic for getting a 'nice few quid' at Exeter after racing.

At that time Exeter had a horseshoe shaped ring with a wire fence to one side of it. Back in those days the bookies used coloured card tickets which were ripped and discarded on the floor when they had been paid. As well as the litter that caused, the bookmakers also used printed sheets of paper for each race with the horse's name, number and later, colours printed on them. These were also just discarded when the race was over. Add to this a whole lot of Sporting Life and Racing Post pages and the ring was a mess. Badger let on that as the books were packing up and punters left, when the wind was right the rubbish was all blown up against the wire fence. Quite often there would be notes in there too, unnoticed by those that had dropped them and other eagle-eyed racegoers. Badger may have been the best but plenty could spot a bank note from a long way off.

This particular day we decided that we would wind Badger up. As soon as the last race was over we kept our eyes open for him, and sure enough we spotted him grabbing a freshly discarded Racing Post from a bin and heading to the fence which was full of wind-blown rubbish. We let him get quite close then got some of our own notes from our pockets and called to him waving the money excitedly with an over the top 'Badger you were right.' His usually jovial face turned to thunder as he used some quite rude words to describe us and vowed he'd never tell us anything again.

I was familiar of course with the two other guys who worked with Jack and Roy but was aware of another through a story I had related to me on occasion when a tall well-built fellow turned up at the joint at Newbury for a chat. 'Big' Shaun had been employed by the Lynns as a floorman stroke body guard. Several years previously Jack had been involved in a betting dispute with an unsavoury character who was rumoured to be a bit of a tasty gypsy fighter type. Jack and Roy stuck to their guns and were backed up with the ring inspector. The gypsy went away empty-handed but left not very veiled threats that the Lynns had better watch their backs.

Others told them that the threat was not to be taken lightly. Bookmakers are pretty safe on racecourses but can be vulnerable in semi-deserted car parks. They decided to take out a bit of insurance and employ a heavyweight in the shape of Shaun. He was taken with them wherever they bet. The gypsy was spotted a few times but despite glaring across the ring a few times he never made any more threats. As the risk from this fellow was assumed to have diminished, so did the days that Shaun was employed, until not before long his services were discreetly no longer required.

Shaun appeared on the racecourse from time to time but I didn't really get to know him until quite a few years later. Even then I didn't get to know him properly but he was on course a lot more as he had gotten involved in a fairly successful syndicate that liked a punt. We got talking one day and he told me that he had done a bit of work for a bookie a long time ago. He added that they just stopped using him but he had no idea why. When I mentioned the gypsy he looked at me blankly so I related the story to him just as it was told to me.

He looked a mixture of confused, then deceived, then just laughed and said, 'The bastards, they never told me!'

In the time working with the Lynns I had the best training possible for the job because they were such hard task masters, you were pretty much under pressure from start to finish on the floor. Then one quiet Bath evening meeting where the going was very fast, so the fields' small, I had the surprise of my life. Roy handed me the pencil and book and informed me that it was time I learned to clerk. There were only tiny fields and I took to it fairly well though was never put under pressure. I never really fancied being the clerk and stuck behind the joint but it was another feather in my cap if I could master it as people were often looking for clerks and paid top wages. As it turned out it was just a one off, at least for the time being.

I was thrown into the deep-end the very next time I was asked to pick up the pencil, on the Wednesday of the Cheltenham festival. John the Postman's wife had committed the cardinal sin of giving birth to their first child on the Tuesday night. I was thrown the pencil and told to get the bets down the best I could which wasn't very well. I did get the bets down but they had no idea where they were and that was no good to a firm that liked to bet tight. Dave Simms was taken from his beloved place on the floor and put in my place once it became apparent that he was actually a top-class clerk. He had kept that from them in the past because he preferred being in the thick of the action rather than under Roy's watchful eye.

# Chapter 5

*The Times They Are A Changing.*

One of the biggest upheavals to hit the betting ring came about in 1992 with the introduction of the extended supplementary list or ESL. This was deemed the end of the world by Jack and Roy. I remember the last meeting before the ESL list came into operation. We were betting at Salisbury. We only ever went there if there was a clash of meetings in our area. As usual we were well down in the poor pitches which were not really viable for run of the mill meetings but if there was a clash with somewhere like Sandown then a few of the London books would be missing and then Jack's seniority came into play so we got move ups. This particular day there was good result after good result and I have a feeling there was an evening meeting that a lot of the books had the option to go to. One by one the layers in front of us left so by the last race there were only 7 bookmakers left in the ring and we bet accordingly. Roy proclaimed that they should make the most of it because it would be the last time it would ever happen. 'The game's really gone now' reinforced John Holland. For a while at least they were both right.

There had been hordes of books chomping at the bit to get off the waiting lists and on to the track to show the existing layers how it was done. Quite a few of them were Silver Ring layers who had started to be there while languishing on the waiting list. It seemed as if they had been stood over in the cheaper enclosure with eyes looking at the perceived greener grass that lay there. The grass was no doubt greener before the new rules, especially when there had been clashes, but the irony of it was that when they all took up the option to fill the vacant pitches those good days no longer existed.

With their number they also brought in the habits of the Silver Ring. The most damaging for the layers but beneficial for the punters was that a lot of them liked to price up a race almost as soon as the runners for the previous race had passed the post. The competition was so fierce for the generally small amounts of money to be taken in the cheaper enclosures that the layers tended to be excellent judges of form and bet to their opinion. When they got into Tattersalls they couldn't wait to get trading and fielding all that money flying around.

To begin with the rest of the ring, the established layers, let them get on with it but soon joined in not bearing the sight of that still limited amount of money going into the back rows. The bigger problems started when two or even more of the new books had a different opinion about a few horses in the same race, so all started to out-price each other betting to smaller and smaller margins way before most layers would have traditionally finished their between-race coffees.

Many of the books that were big fish in the Silver Ring were determined to be so in Tatts and very determined to take all they could and prove that they too could have always been high-rollers were they not treated with such exclusion over all those years. The punters couldn't believe their luck while the books in the established pitches just looked on with a mixture of horror and disbelief. At first they had the luxury of being able to lay their regular punters and then get the bet back with the heroes behind them at bigger prices. That honeymoon period didn't last long as they soon discovered that punter loyalty lasted as long as the prices on respective boards and that the books behind suddenly finding they were being tucked up by the clever people with nowhere to go.

The books in the established pitches had no option but to batten down the hatches and try to take advantage of their superior positions while those who had no idea of value knock themselves out. For people like the Lynns it was a very difficult time because their pitches were still bad but they never had the respite of a clash meeting where they could get good value with not many other layers in the ring. One seasoned layer likened those coming into the ring on the ESL (some unknown to anyone) to Indians in an old Hollywood western. Every time the cowboys think they have seen off the last of them another lot come over the horizon.

One consequence of the ESL is that we started to go to regional Point-to-Points more often instead of regular race meetings. Jack had been going to points for years but had forsaken them in recent seasons when the business on racecourses had been good during the boom times of the 1980s. They had kept them up attending the correct amount of meetings but were far from regulars as the pickings, although there for the taking, were modest. The points were run on a similar way to the racecourse waiting lists, but a 'pick' order as opposed to positions. This was because point layouts often changed, indeed as did the venue. The other difference, most importantly for this story is that the ESL rule hadn't been adopted.

For some years those books on the waiting list could pretty much guess correctly the bookies who would not be attending so would take the gamble of turning up to be in the vacant spaces. The gamble was that if a pitch holder did turn up then they would have had a wasted journey. There were some dark looks from some firms when we arrived unexpectedly to small points when everyone had expected that we'd be somewhere like Chepstow.

Despite being the pitch-holder some people despised the racecourse books turning up to bet when they could have been at a proper racecourse and the person they stopped betting had no other option. The Devon and Cornwall point to points actually had a very strong bunch of bookmakers. The main layers from Tattersalls were in evidence at the bigger points. Dave Pipe, Harry Metcalfe, Bernard Redfern, David Phillips, Matt Green all had pitches as did a lot of established books from the silver ring. There were a few specialist point bookmakers too.

The system for laying out the pitches involved a rope with bits of string or tape marking out equally spaced positions. The bookmaker would pick in order and claim their stake by pegging in their joints with all sorts of elaborate methods. Big spikes, hooks and tent-pegs were all used to keep the joints, the umbrellas that used to act as kites in blustery weather, and the rest of the kit in place. Each firm with their own tried and tested, though time consuming methods.

One particular venue was always good value for fun and games. The point at Ottery St Mary was owned by successful, although eccentric, owner-trainer Oliver Carter, who would make it his mission to upset the bookies as often as possible during the day. One of his favourites was to wait until all the banging and clanging of pitch erection had been completed, then march up and demand that the line was moved, quite often just a couple of feet either way. He owned the land so what he said went. He was also very fond of making announcements, largely inaudible over the PA system. Quite often these would relate to litter, urging the public and the bookies to put their rubbish in the big oil drums provided. It was a common sight to see a white coat clad Oliver marching from the second last holding aloft a betting card, although obviously discarded by a losing punter he would take issue with the bookie whose name was on it as if it was his fault. It was all good fun in hindsight but a royal pain in the arse at the time. People were wise to him though. On at least one occasion nobody moved anything, but were greeted with a 'That's better' half an hour later when he came back to inspect.

The point to point punters were soon familiar, so much so that a lot of bookies hardly issued a ticket, preferring instead to put the bet down to a name in the book. Of course this saved on tickets but also the punters definitely liked the personal touch. Quite often the bookie would know the name of the punter so it would be down to Dave, Brian or Bill but more often than not the face would be familiar but the name had escaped, so in haste, something like hat, stick or farmer would be used. The latter was a fairly tricky one, because being at point to points 'farmer' was quite a well-used moniker. It was OK while getting the bets down but confusion reigned when it came to paying out. The question how much does farmer want would be greeted by silence as the clerk looked at a field book with enough farmers in it to keep 'Country File' busy for a decade followed by a 'Which bloody farmer?'

When the weather was good point to points could be a lovely way to spend an afternoon but when it was cold and wet it was miserable. There were some points where the weather was so bad and the mud so deep that tractors were actually towing cars onto the course before racing, not just off afterwards.

One other difference from racing on racecourses was that the fields only became known 40 minutes before the race. The racecard would hold every potential runner then the numbers man would come around and give the huddle of bookmakers' floormen the numbers. If too many horses had been entered for the race then it would be split. That may have been music to the ears when the crowd was big with business to match but dreaded when it was cold and wet. The last thing you wanted to hear was 'They have split the maiden.' The most races run in a day that I can remember was 13. In truth the punters were only there in any number for the first six or seven races. After that it was the connections that wanted to back their fancied horses left later on, especially if the weather was miserable. The remaining races that had been split would often be maidens so the layers had to have their wits about them, as did the floormen. In these events at first glance it looked as if the books had generally bet to good margins but in reality they only laid the fancied horses.

Legend has it that on one particular afternoon the line of layers had gone through a torrid time of punts being landed and favourites going in one after the other. Bernard Redfern had the needle so in the last race of unraced maidens he chalked up even money every horse in the race. 'Go on then take your pick' he bellowed to the handful of punters still remaining. They say the stampede that followed was a cracker despite the relatively few participants; they all wanted to be on the same horse and continued to back it at all rates down. Bernard had bet to about 500% and just had the one loser, that won by half the track.

Another story that was related to me goes back in the mists of time. It is said that the weather was atrocious and that one by one the bookmakers either quit betting because they were fed up with it or had to because the clerks books were soaked and the bookies' tickets all mashed together. By the last race the rain was howling and the wind blowing a gale. All the bookmakers had taken refuge in the nearby beer tent, all except one. This was not unusual for the bookie in question as he was notoriously mean, from not giving his staff any sort of bonus, to laying skinny odds and bluffing bets wherever he could. There were only five horses in the race so the bookmaker decided he would stand there and take on all-comers even though it was impossible to keep prices on the board because of the rain. So there he stood all huddled under his umbrella. It is said that one by one the connections of the horses went to enquire about a price, each was laid, to sizeable amounts to very skinny odds. The punters were happy to get on and the bookie couldn't believe his luck, he had a good betting race to himself. He hadn't let on to the other punters the prices he had laid but it was rumoured he'd averaged them around 5/4 each.

As the last punter trudged from his joint the bookmaker was seen to shove a wad of notes into his jacket and jump down onto the sodden ankle-deep mud with a massive smile on his face. He marched purposefully into the packed tent and then stunned everyone by ordering a round for all, which depending on whom you listen to ranged from 20-40 people. All those that knew the usual frugal nature of the layer are said to have ordered doubles or pints with chasers to make up for all the times that they had been bluffed, knocked back, or in the case of his astonished, sodden and for this race redundant clerk, not bunged on good days. He paid the not unsubstantial amount over to the man behind the bar and then announced to all his 'foolish' fellow bookmakers who had not bet on the race that he was 'overs' for several hundred pounds so the best he could do was buy them all a drink.

Of course he had to do this because he had to let everyone know how clever he had been and how foolish everyone else was, part of the winning was the joy of gloating. As all around were sinking their doubles to ease the pain of being ridiculed suddenly the tent bust open letting the wind howl in and the rain soak all those within its range as the numbers runner ran in. The looks of annoyance all turned to that of joy and mirth as he'd panted breathlessly 'They've abandoned the last.' All stakes refunded then.

Just one more story displayed the dark humour though sometimes maybe the comment wasn't totally a joke. A fairly big punter/owner had gone down the line backing his horse at a local point. His horse had won fairly easily so he rushed back into the ring to wind up the bookies. He went to the first in the line and drew a bundle of cash before heading off to the winner's enclosure to get his trophy. Not long afterwards the ashen-faced numbers man came back to report that the guy had died, dropped dead of a heart attack while being presented his trophy. There was a hush, but one bookmaker seemed to be much more upset than the others. They all knew the man as he was a regular. Noticing this, a punter asked if he was a special friend or related, 'No' replied the layer, 'I'm the only one he drew off before he pegged it.'

Some point to points were very popular, especially bank holiday meetings. Those were the days when the bookies could bet to huge margins and take bets for most of the field then it would be almost the fabled 'License to print money' where they could bet overs every race. One particular day was so good that Roy sat in the front of the car with his arms hod deep into the satchel and just threw notes into the air proclaiming 'They just gave it to us dad, gave it to us.'

There were occasions when the firm did take a bit of a risk but I can count those on two fingers. Funnily enough they were both at Salisbury. The first was quite early on when I worked for them. In those days there was a pitch all out on a limb at the corner of the stand. It wasn't very good in the bigger scheme of things but better than any of our pitches we generally bet in. Totally out of character for the firm Roy went best price the favourite and gave it the stripe. I told them they were best price the horse so many times that I was called over and told through gritted teeth that 'He knew.' They must have stood the horse for a fortune in their way of doing things. The favourite was the first one beaten. Roy stood on the joint just below the punters and put his arm in the air. Then it became apparent that not only was the favourite beaten but a total rag was going to win the race, the arm went back up again with a hearty 'Go on my cocker.'

I can still see the punters who had to a man all done their money, at least with us, scowling down at him. It was smiles all around on the firm as we immediately packed up to leave. They remained very tight-lipped about why they had stuck their necks out with the horse but evidently had their card well and truly marked. The second occasion wasn't so happy. One thing we always noticed was that ladies loved to back any horse that had some sort of sexual double entendre to it. Roy couldn't stop laying a horse despite being well under the odds. I told him he could hedge it back bigger but he said that the horse had no chance and that they were just betting the name. The form books will relate that the race was won by the unconsidered 20/1 shot, Spunky. I can also relate that the journey home was a very quiet one.

Jack used to pick me up and drive to meet Roy a few miles further up the M5. He had an old Jaguar that he used to steer with serene elegance at a steady pace. We used to get on really well and chat about all sorts on that short trip up the motorway. His advice was pretty much always non P.C. but I always enjoyed hearing it. Whereas we were always setting the world to rights, one particular day ours almost came to an untimely end. We were driving up the motorway in really filthy weather; pouring rain making visibility bad enough then lorries were throwing up spray making things even worse. The slow lane was full with HGVs so Jack made cautious progress overtaking them in the middle lane when all of a sudden a pair of brake lights blazed on in front of us. I think Jack and I slammed out feet on the brakes simultaneously, luckily his hit the pedals and were effective whereas mine just hurt my knees. Before we knew it the Jag was in a full skid turning anti-clockwise, I waited with horror as the car span so we could have a view of where we had not been going and braced myself fully expecting to see the lights of an articulated lorry bearing down to splat us into oblivion.

Lady Luck was looking down favourably on us that day for sure. Rather than instant death facing us there wasn't another car in sight as we came to a halt straddling the inside line and the hard-shoulder. So empty infact that Jack managed to do a quick manoeuvre and get us back on the road and moving again. We were both quite shaken but decided we'd keep the incident to ourselves mentioning nothing of it to Roy when we reached our rendezvous. Our eventual destination was Newbury, where we bet in the rain and everything went horribly wrong as far as taking bets went. We had used up our portion of luck for at least one day. While Roy was getting into more and more of a stew and flap, Jack remained tranquillity personified, 'We need a result, badly' barked Roy before slamming the book to the floor as yet another favourite just got up on the line to foil the outsider that looked certain to win. Jack looked at me and whispered 'We daren't tell him we've already had the double result up this morning.' He was right there.

Although the relationship with the Lynns was a very good one, things often got fraught during the racing. Some bookies remained placid win or lose, though it has to be said not all that many, while others were wound up to the max. Roy Lynn was one of those in the latter. It's a high pressure game racing and he was like a cooker of the same name ready to blow on occasion.

I had often had to have a thick skin and tell myself that it was all said in the heat of the moment, but there were plenty of times that I told myself that if he shouts just once more I'm off. One day it came to that. We were betting at Taunton on a miserable cold and wet day at the end of February. The rain had been pouring down the whole day and everyone was soaked. Worse than people being soaked, card tickets and field books were getting soggy and pens were being swapped for pencils just to be able to get the bets down.

As business had been quite poor I had been having quite a lot of smallish back bets as Roy strove to keep his book tidy as usual. The problem for me was that my racecard and old piece of number sheet that I had been using to record them was rapidly turning into illegible papier-mâché. I had them in my head but the usual routine of crossing the bets out as I paid them was going out of the window. One of the bookmakers I bet back with was an elderly Welsh layer Benny Edwards. I can't remember the exact bet but it was something like a £100-£12. The firm was a well-respected and professional one but like everyone else the smooth running was being scuppered by the inclement weather.

I had been told from an early stage with the Lynns that whenever possible always pay the clerk and make sure he crosses the bet out in the book. I always tried to do that, and went to the clerk on the Benny Edwards joint. They were in the process of having a right ruck. Benny was shouting at the floorman and calling bets at the same time. The clerk was trying to pay out but had to keep turning soggy pages blowing in the icy wind and getting annoyed that his boss was calling bets in so early, before everyone had been paid out. I paid the clerk which only made him even stroppier . He took the money as he battled with the elements, bets and holding his hat on, but paid he was.

I got back to watching the floor and giving the Lynns shows then all of a sudden I heard my name screamed, I peered over to see two faces looking darker than the leaden skies above. Roy was looked like a bulldog who had been chewing a wasp before falling into a river and Benny was doing a very good impression of Roy. 'You haven't paid Benny' screamed Roy. I protested that I had, but Roy wasn't listening, took the amount Benny said that I owed from the pound coins (must have had too many) squared him up (again) and apologised to him.

Then, much to the delight of the small line of punters either waiting to be paid or to get on, Roy launched into a full frontal verbal assault on me. He was screaming how I had always been told to pay the clerk, why couldn't I just do a simple job so on and so on and so on. I had to put up with being shouted at like that in the Army but didn't really appreciate it in Civvy Street, after all I had done my time. By this point the whole public humiliation was getting more public, both Dave Phillips and Dave Parsons had stopped to watch. One thing I did learn in the Army was to let it go over your head, especially when losing your rag wasn't really an option. I was in full, 'look at the badge on the Sergeant Major's beret' mode as Roy screamed abuse, then one of the punters laughed. That was it.

I asked Roy if he had finished, turned and walked to where I had been before being called over. Roy had already seemingly forgotten about it and was taking bets and paying out the fully entertained punter. Rather than carry on with my work I walked to where I had been but kept walking, past the last bookmaker, past the gates, past the carpark, out of the racecourse and towards the motorway, thumb out for a lift.

Apparently I wasn't missed for a while, then the familiar cry of 'Simon!' rang out, followed by Roy rushing around looking for me. Of course, nothing gets missed in a racecourse betting ring so it wasn't long before someone let him know that I was last seen exiting stage left.

I got home in double-quick time having been spotted by some Tiverton locals and was soon reflecting on having thrown away the opportunity to go racing on a regular basis. I need not have worried, as it wasn't long before I got a phone call from another bookmaker asking if I had left and was available for work. Suddenly it dawned on me that I was in fact a valued member of the betting ring community and that my services were required. I had obviously impressed at least one other bookie despite being shouted at and made fun of on a regular basis. The next phone call I got was from the Lynns, very apologetic and asking me back. Both of us had cooled down and I agreed, not least because Cheltenham was just around the corner, something I suspected had been on both our minds.

# Chapter 6

*Moving On, David Phillips Of Torquay.*

I continued to work for the Lynns until the summer of 1995 but then gave up the whole scene and England and moved to Germany for the summer to live and work with friend in a band I drove for at the time. There are enough tales there to fill another book, watch this space. When I came back Roy Lynn's son had taken my position on a full time basis which of course was fair enough. It wasn't long before I had a phone call from my next regular bookmaker, David Phillips.

David was based in Torquay and friendly with the Lynns so he was familiar with me. I was always impressed by his very laid-back attitude and astute way of betting. He also went further afield than the Lynns, exotic places like Windsor, Worcester and Fontwell. I had done the odd day's work with him when working with the Lynns and enjoyed it. Life was a whole lot easier with Dave and with no disrespect to the former, he was a good student of form and would bet according to his opinion as opposed to the Lynns who were basically excellent bookies that worked to figures. Dave's way of playing meant that days became a whole lot more exciting. Quite often we would tip-toe around, not really trying too hard on races then, bam, we would be going down the book with a favourite, ducking a horse or going for it.

One aspect of working for Dave that differed from the previous firm was that he used to take Neil Wilkins' tissue. This meant you would all get in a huddle before racing and mark down what he supposed the market would be along with some C for careful for horses he had heard the whisper about. This really made me feel part of the 'scene.' He only operated these tissues in the London area which was a place where I never felt all that at home. This meant interaction with some of the other floormen and a little bit of 'inside' info when those 'C's proliferated the card. Despite being slightly more 'accepted' in the ring simply by getting these and paying Neil the couple of quid a day it cost, you also got the impression that the guy reading them out at super-rapid pace was doing it in the hope that he'd leave you behind and make a point of stopping just for you. Luckily I was generally a quick scribbler down of prices and 'C's. Neil was an SP reporter, running the team that reported on live market movements and collected the big bets so was well-known and liked by the bookies. He made a great impression on me, always dressed immaculately and smoking outsized cigars. OK, the latter didn't impress me much but he made a striking figure about the ring.

One chap who caused mirth and frustration in equal measure that I came into a lot more contact with because we frequented the London tracks was the fellow who dished out the sheets with the runners and colours on. He was a tall gangling guy who was 'Millwall through and through' and appeared to have a real distain for anyone who wasn't from London or at least wasn't a front-line bookie. He would walk along the line handing out these sheets.

Some firms just put the sheets straight into their joints, but others like the Lynns and us put a whole host of information on them. One of my jobs was to go through the card and mark important info on the sheet in pencil under the horses' names. For example, any 'careful' that Neil Wilkins' card might have thrown up, Martin Pipe, Henry Cecil, Barney Curley etc. We'd also put the tissue price and in the case of places like Goodwood over 7f where the draw was important, that too. It's OK to say now that everyone has light boards but had punters had a good look at our sheets they would have got a wealth of information. Anyway, back to the whole point of this paragraph, Del, was an objectionable bugger. If you saw him up at the other end of the ring stopping to chat with everyone he knew, which appeared to be most people, you knew it was going to be a while before he got down to you. The sensible thing was to go up and politely ask him for the sheet so that you could get on with your markings.

Del would either stand there and look at you with a one-toothed open-mouthed look of mock outrage that you had the audacity to interrupt his conversation about last night's game or he'd look from side to side for added affect to see if anyone around had noticed this Oliver-like character who was asking for something out of turn. If you were lucky he'd then thrust a set of sheets into your hand warning you that you should wait your turn in future and follow it up with a look to the sky and a further exaggerated look around.

If you weren't lucky, and that was a shade of odds-on, he'd tell you that you had to wait your turn as he was giving them out in order. In order was particularly annoying, especially at places like Royal Ascot and you bet on the end of the third row where he would walk past you twice, with a good 10 minutes between each lap. Even more annoying was seeing one of his mates come running down and ask for their sheets out of turn and getting one.

The whole comical scenario was exacerbated when he would come around for his £9. He would expect you to say keep the pound. Of course we had the right hump with him by that time so we quite often waited for the change. This would have him grumbling no end and ensure we had to wait until the last minute the following day because he wouldn't forget. The trouble was, he would forget if we decided on biting the bullet and bunging him the extra pound, the next day it was still the same. At the time I just thought he was an awkward bloke who was making the most of his little bit of power but much later on I got to know him and found him to be a lovely bloke who appeared to have a proper wicked sense of humour and was having a joke on us.

There was another guy who was always collecting money. This one was exclusively at Newbury. He'd come around at every meeting asking for £2 for 'cloakroom.' We had no idea what he was talking about but were pretty certain that the cloakroom no longer existed. We certainly didn't use one or ever give him the money. Undaunted he'd still come around every meeting and ask for the £2. Weirdly, it seemed that a lot of the books around us just fished the money out of the smash tray and paid him. I can only guess that he had being doing it for years and the books had simply forgotten who he was and why they were paying him. Give him his due though, he'd even sometimes come up and have £2 on one with us no doubt in an attempt to win us over. I'm not sure if he died or his scam died when the new blood flooded the ring but he appeared to vanish along with the old stand.

There was another character, or at least bet, unique to Newbury, where there is a landing and take-off strip in the centre of the course. As a plane was doing either and you were near enough to bookie Bobby Mack's joint you'd hear him calling 'Take 100/1, Take 100/1' in other words you could bet at 1/100 that the plane would land or take off safely. He used to always say that he'd cop one day, not that I ever saw anyone take advantage of what was no doubt a value bet. I wasn't at the track the day there was a tragic crash. You like to think he hadn't done any business on it.

David had a fairly loose group of people that worked for him as and when he needed them. They included retired people, other bookmakers and Trevor Taylor, ex British Commonwealth table-tennis champion and close friend of Martin Pipe's sidekick Chester Barnes. The pair used to tour holiday camps and gave demonstrations of their skills and went back years. Trevor was a wizard with the form book but a miniscule if prolific punter. He claimed that the Pipes asked his advice before making purchases on occasion. When I learned this I hoped that maybe he would be the golden goose that was going to lay nuggets of red hot Pipe info. Sadly, this was not the case.

While he was an expert with the form book Trevor wasn't the best floorman in the world. He was quite often more preoccupied with his own bets than doing the job but we had fun with this. At Worcester he would be sent with a walkie-talkie into the then still vibrant Silver Ring for hedging purposes.

He'd be easy to spot because he wore an omnipresent blue cagoule, even in the summer, so stood out quite well. The Silver Ring was on the other side of the track from where we were betting and boasted a Tote betting shop as well as a row of bookies. The betting shop was at the top of half a dozen or so steps. As the start of an away race, that we suspected Trevor might have an interest in, approached we'd see him make his vantage point higher and higher up the stairs. At first his head would dart around once or twice to see what was going on. Then he would be fully engrossed in watching whatever was unfolding inside then when he could bear it no longer would nip into the shop and disappear completely.

It would be at this point that we would have a chuckle at Trevor's expense and ask him the price of a certain horse in the ring. More often than not he would duck out and have a look, answer the question and duck back in again. That would depend on how near his race was to the business end. If it was quite near he'd either not hear the radio genuinely, or pretend not to, then come rushing out.

Not only was Trevor's cagoule an easy way of spotting him locally but it also made national TV. Unknown to Trevor I had applied to go on BBC TV's morning show 'Style Challenge.'

It was a programme where they got people on the show looking very scruffy. They were made over and then blindfolded, dressed, and stood in front of life sized mirrors, had the blindfold removed, the mirror was spun around and hey presto, you looked a million quid. It was a while before I heard anything but then had a phone call out of the blue asking if Trevor and I could attend an audition in Plymouth. That is when I supposed that I had better tell him. I didn't hold out much hope that he would agree. He wasn't keen but then I pointed out that the contestants got to keep their clobber, which was generally around a monkey so he reluctantly agreed to come to the audition.

We got through the audition, much to the amazement of Trev who confided later that he had done his level best to make sure we didn't. We were offered train tickets up to Birmingham and a hotel after the recording but Trev said he'd rather drive. I foolishly went out and had a few beers the night before so was feeling a little peaky when he picked me up. I was still feeling much the same when we arrived at the studio.

The show was recorded in threes and ours was to be the last one. First things first we were separated and taken down a large corridor and into a windowless room and asked to wait. A few minutes later a gaggle of women came and introduced themselves then told me strip down to my boxers. This would normally have been a rather excellent invitation but in this scenario was rather intimidating as I stood there feeling decidedly flabby and wishing I'd stuck to my proposed gym routine rather than go to the pub.

I made a rather lame apology for being fat then felt even worse when told that they could cover a multitude of sins. The next thing I knew I was blindfolded and then dressed and undressed while the ladies discussed the best outfit for me. Next I was introduced to an unseen hairdresser who proclaimed that only once in his entire hairdressing career had he seen hair in such bad condition. Then came a very camp skincare expert who veritably shrieked in horror 'Oh my God he's got a spot.' It was true I did and I wasn't too happy about that either but it was supposed to be a challenge after all.

Once everyone was happy my blindfold was removed and I was invited to get dressed again. The next couple of hours were spent in the audience suffering the worst hangover in the world, trying not to be sick and wondering if Trev was going to up and leave at any minute. When our time came it was more of a relief than excitement but was great fun. Trev was given the full treatment, cucumber in the eyes, full shave. I was on the receiving end of a quite drastic haircut and full facial including some sort of acid dropped on the spot that deeply offended the skin guy. The whole show was punctuated with racing puns and mentions.

When the mirrors span around I was dressed more as a stereotypical second-hand car dealer than a bookie but apart from the clutch bag it was all clobber that I would and did wear, pin-striped suit, overcoat, the lot. Trev looked a changed man, leather sports coat, smart slacks and clean shaven. His stuff was rumoured to have been available to bid for on eBay the very next morning. He was indeed a trend horse.

Another chap that Dave used to employ on a regular basis was fellow bookmaker and long-time excellent clerk whose name we shortened to the initials PB whenever we wanted to address him. He was a very lovely fellow who literally wouldn't say boo to a goose and was methodical and diligent, just what you need from a clerk. Nobody that knew him could find argument with the way I have just described him but it has to be said he had another trait. He was very, let's say, careful. He told me on numerous occasions that when a bookmaker offers you something for free you should always take it and that that rule should always be adhered to even if you didn't really want what they were offering. So you name it he'd take it, a cup of tea after he had just drained his flask, sandwich when he'd just eaten, and if he could get away with it, the most expensive item on the menu when staying away.

Of course all those things he was entitled to but his frugal ways were a standing joke on the firm. One of his favourite pastimes was going into Tesco minutes before closing time, before these days of 24 hour opening, and buying up all the reduced to clear items. The genius stroke would then be if any of them weren't up to scratch he'd write to the company complaining. We were often regaled with tales of victory with letters of apology containing vouchers for £2. It was the norm that if we stayed away the boss would pay for the accommodation and take us out for a meal and a couple of pints. It was also the norm that we would probably get our round back. The standing joke was that PB wouldn't spend anything at all throughout the week. He would have a very hearty breakfast and then starve all day unless something was bought for him then fill up again with the evening meal before ducking out before the rounds started.

One particular Glorious Goodwood we were staying in Worthing at a traditional bed and breakfast run by a lady with a penchant for cats. It has to be said that the boss hadn't exactly pushed the boat out for a week-long stay. Just for fun his son and I decided to have a spread bet on how much PB was going to spend all week. The trouble was as the agreed spread was zero there wasn't much room for manoeuvre unless you wanted to buy, and nobody wanted to do that. I had to share with PB. Our tiny single beds were end to end in a room so small that the corners touched. The other feature of the room was a TV, which apart from being ancient also had a meter on it. It would have been impossible for both of us to watch the TV without sitting too close for comfort on one bed so I gave it, and the one pound slot a miss.

By the end of the week it was agreed that we could go on

a firm night out as we had spotted a local nightclub. PB didn't fancy it. He didn't fancy the night club anyway and he definitely didn't fancy how much it was going to cost. The alternative was going to be sat in that crypt-like room with no TV. My task on our return was to see if he had actually spent a pound to watch it. The fact that he hadn't asked to borrow one made us think that he'd not succumb to the temptation. Not that he was by any means skint but thought maybe that he'd take the extra precaution of not bringing any money just in case such a temptation were put before him. That proved to be one step too far, even for PB. He must have had a closely guarded emergency stash because when we returned from a slightly boozy, but otherwise uneventful, night out he was fast asleep with the TV still flickering a late night channel.

Some other firms used to have a much more raucous time than us when they went out. One firm from Yeovil were notorious for their hard raging every night especially at festival meetings. One story that endures is that after a particularly heavy night on the booze the staff all went in their own direction. One member admitted that the events of the evening after a certain point are not just vague but are blank. He was in a comfortable booze laden slumber when he was rudely awakened by a piercing scream. He leapt out of his sleep with a start and was amazed to find that he had just landed fully-clothed in what appeared to be a hotel corridor in front of an extremely shaken cleaning lady.

He had evidently not been able to find his room so decided to sleep in an unlocked laundry cupboard. On realising his predicament he made his apologies and made off, rummaging for his key as he went. Things went from bad to worse when he got to the room number that was on his key only for it not to fit. He marched down to reception to complain, only to discover that not only had he not made it to his room, he had not made it to the right hotel either. The story has been verified by all concerned. It's just that those concerned aren't admitting which one of them it was. One wag suggested that it's not beyond the realms of possibility that it has happened to both of them at independent times.

Another Goodwood the boss thought that he had cracked it for the accommodation, an adults-only holiday camp on Hayling Island. I think he had some sort of mental image of a slightly older 18-30s resort with all night dancing and loads of party fun with hen and stag nights running amok. Whatever he imagined those illusions were immediately shattered when we checked in. From the foyer we could hear dusty old ballroom music and even worse, to our horror we could see an extremely old lady being waltzed around the dance floor in her wheelchair by an even older (if that was possible) old lady. It soon dawned on us that rather than being a happening vibrant adults-only environment we had booked into some sort of very nice place favoured by the over 70s.

For dinner in true holiday camp style we had set tables. We had to share with a lovely old couple who were celebrating their 60th wedding anniversary. They were very sparky and with it. Too 'with it' as it happened and totally off the mark. It became quite apparent they assumed that we were a gay couple. Not that either of us are at all homophobic but on the other hand male machismo ensured that we spent the rest of the week talking in deep voices about women an awful lot. In hindsight it would have been funnier to ham it up and go along with it.

Of the places I used to go with Dave, that I hadn't done with the Lynns that I really loved was Windsor on Monday nights. I hadn't been since that Monday night when stood next to Barney Curley when Eternal Triangle got the better of Tyrnippy, back when I was in the army. The racecourse had an old-world charm about it, was buzzing with plenty of bookmakers and punters and had a really nice atmosphere.

Betting there was totally different to most other places we worked at, for several reasons. The fields were often large and the punters seemed to be enthusiastic novices with plenty of money.

It was a regular occurrence there that a young city type would stroll up to the joint with a lady on his arm and ask for a swathe of pony or fifty pound bets each way and then ask his companion what she would like then have a couple more with similar sums. The books we would have would feature some big losers but the theory was that the people who were betting with you were just guessing. The odds were in our favour and the racing was competitive so we'd let them make our book. Over a period of time we were certain to beat them. The racing was very exciting for that reason. You might have a 14 runner handicap with 3 losing you a nice few quid so had plenty to will back and cheer on.

Of course there were several times when we caught a cold and the punters got it right, but there was no way they could win in the long run and business was good enough for the law of averages to swing back in our favour, where the odds always were of course. Needless to say there were plenty of sharks about too so you had to have your wits about you.

Sometimes those sharks were us, or at least we were attempting to be. The boss really fancied a 16/1 shot one day, he sent me out into the silver ring, which was very vibrant at the time, with some readies and told me to get as much of it as I could on at that price or bigger. I loved that type of task. The reason I had cash was in the hope that I would sneak in under the radar. I was told not to even ask for fractions because that would look too professional. When I got through the gate I noticed that our fancy was 20/1 and 25/1 in a place. The bookmaker going the biggest price was a layer I had seen before in the Midlands rings. He would have been a big fish out here so decided to ask for £40 each way at 25/1, a big mistake. He glared down at me and shouted that I had a tenner each-way and should be happy with that, before pointing down and bellowing 'Don't think we don't know who you are!' As far as I was concerned I was nobody, but his outburst was enough for the price to disappear all around the ring. I scuttled back to boss with my tail between my legs, but at least I had proof that I'd got some 'pony', and was walking just a little bit taller in the knowledge that I had put the fear of God into Windsor Silver Ring. The horse didn't though; the boss's judgement was well adrift with the horse running a stinker.

The author with Jack Lynn.

Clockwise from top left :
- A Devon Point to Point, far from the glamour of Ascot
- In recent years things have become a bit lonely at times
- The other end of the scale, high-rolling rails layer Geoff Banks does battle at Royal Ascot

Clockwise from top:
- 'Geordie'
- The author, Army days, surrounded with racing paraphernalia
- The author and 'Big Mac', 28 years after the autograph

From top to bottom:
- Newton Abbot
- Bath Tatts, back row betting, 2002
- Exeter, late 1980's
- Winning Post, Kempton

Clockwise, from top left:
- Cheltenham Festival Betting Ring
- Chepstow, 1980's
- The author, John Mackie Yard
- Point to Point, 1990's
- Bath Tatts, 2002

Clockwise, from top left:
- 'Balertwine Barry
- Point to Point, 1990's, Dave Phillips
- The author, 'Racing Winker', Bath, 2000's
- Long suffering staff like 'Mossy' still have to eat

Clockwise, from top left:
- Ian Metcalfe braves the elements with a smile
- Brian Edwards and Ivor Perry
- Ivor Perry, Point to Point
- Jim Clarke and Andrew Mount sort out a winner
- Ivor Perry with author in background

Clockwise, from top left:
- Jack Lynn and 'Balertwine' Barry
- Pete 'the Punter' and bookies Jack Lynn and Kenny Wager
- Roy and Jack Lynn

Clockwise, from top left:
- Paul Metcalfe and 'Johnny Boy'
- The clerk and the pencil, John White
- The author, Newton Abbot
- Martyn gets to work at Cheltenham

From top to bottom:
- The author in clobber from BBC TV's 'Style Challenge'
- The author, Exeter, 1989

# Chapter 7

*Adventures At The Grand National.*

I was extremely pleased when the boss bought a pitch at Liverpool. It was valid just for the Saturday of the Grand National. I had never been to the meeting so was very excited at the prospect of seeing the great race in the flesh. We were to bet on the embankment which was down by the start of the race near the usually dramatic first and second fences. It was also the cheapest enclosure at the course. The pitch has previously been worked by an ageing silver ring firm and was according to them, maybe not surprisingly, a 'goldmine.' It was ideal for the boss. He was going to enjoy the day out too and being a position that is only used the one day of the year there was no onus to make that long journey more than once annually.

As word got around that Dave had bought the pitch other rumours about the 'goldmine' came out, more like a gold rush in the Wild West was one opinion. Apparently although there was undoubtedly a large crowd out there they were according to some, drunken hooligans all. Add to that aggressive and thieving and you get the picture that was being painted for us. Most of the stories about bookies getting rushed and their hods dipped or gangs of hard-cases flash mobbing a pitch with a fabricated dispute and intimidating the firm into coughing up a sum of money in fear of their lives were third hand. Even though obviously told with a little bit of devilment in mind they patently preyed on the boss's mind. He did his best to give the impression that he had shrugged it all off. After all, the firm that sold it must have had a combined age of 400 years and had probably worked the pitch for 100 of them so it couldn't be that bad.

On the eve of our first trip up to Liverpool it appeared that it could, or at least it had been on the boss's mind enough to give me a call. Tiverton had long-since had a reputation for harbouring its fair share of yobbos, at least for a small market town, so that is why he thought of me. Not for my street-fighting prowess, hell no. I'm 5' 7' in my socks but always found it easy to get on well with the town's hard nuts. That was the talent he was after. He wanted to know if I knew a 'Reliable hard bastard that wouldn't steal from us and knew a bit about racing.' Anyone who met the criteria was to be asked if they'd like to come to the Grand National 1996 and work on the joint for a day.

I did know a few such fellows. Most of the Tiverton toughs around my age would have a punt in between their pints on a Saturday, that was enough to know about horseracing the boss told me. The one I asked was the hardest case in town. He was one of the volatile ones who was friendly enough to me on most occasions but you wouldn't take liberties with him because you were still just as likely to get a smack around the chops if you said something out of turn. I saw this as a great opportunity to get in the tough guy's good books a little bit more and thus protect my safety in Tiverton's rougher drinking establishments in the future. My theory did seem to be barking up the right tree when the guy I had in mind was extremely excited to be asked. He was pretty chuffed when he got the full story that he was there as protection as well as giving change and was ready at the allotted time very early on the Saturday morning. He was dressed to the nines, suit and tie with a very smart raincoat. He sat in the front with the boss and elected to keep his coat on despite the boss suggesting as it was a long journey he might be more comfortable with it off.

On the journey up to Liverpool the allotted hard-man told a fair few stories about how often he had been to the races and of his betting successes. Obvious to the boss and me that they were being embroidered somewhat, but not to worry. It was his brick shit-house presence and hopefully amiable attitude that was needed. We stopped for a fry-up on the way up. The coat didn't come off but the breakfast gratefully accepted and eagerly scoffed. My first sight of the approach to Aintree was a bit of a shock to all of us. The road was full of shops, all metal-shuttered and closed and had a grass verge running down the centre of it, strewn with rubbish. This quite desolate scene was a little alarming and I for one was glad to have brought our Tiverton protection. Having said that though I think being miles outside of our comfort zone and heads filled with horror stories had affected us more than it should have. After all this was the world's most famous horserace, not held at some gypsy flapping track.

We had been advised that we would be better off paying to park in a nearby working mens' club and walking the short distance to our enclosure to aid a quick getaway after racing. We followed instructions, paid the fiver and parked the car. The boss and I started unpacking the kit while our passenger shifted around looking uncomfortable, hardly surprising after being sat in the car for the best part of five hours with a raincoat on. He grimaced a bit and reached into the inside of his pocket, rummaged around a bit then to my horror and the bosses utter astonishment pulled out a large rubber cosh saying 'Oh that's better, this bastard has been sticking in my ribs for fucking miles.' It was an horrendous freeze-frame type moment where I was unsure what was going to happen next. He broke the silence by re-sheathing his weapon with an 'Oh that's better' before returning to the passenger seat to get his bag. We dared not ask what was in there.

The boss looked at me with a look of total surprise which transformed into a beaming smile with a thumbs up. The day itself was a lot less interesting. The pitch itself was so poor that the boss decided to send me into the main ring and clerk himself while our club wielding pal took the bets. Rough Quest won the Grand National. There was no hint of aggro. We got a few quid in front and left before the last. Mission accomplished with no bloodshed, robbery or intimidation.

The following year it was decided that we didn't need a bodyguard so took a regular team. Things started well until an announcement was made that there had been a warning about a bomb planted on course. We were told that the racecourse had to be evacuated; we were to leave all of our kit and just go so that the racecourse could be searched. Most people did exactly as they were told and just removed their money from their hods and left expecting to return in a few minutes. Given my old army experience I pointed out to the boss that if they were taking the bomb alert seriously there was no way that we would be racing that day.

The kit was just a tripod and hod so we packed it up. After all it would have taken just a few minutes to put it back up had I been wrong, and left. By the time we got to the car it became obvious that there was chaos. Local householders were already brewing cups of tea for people. The boss made a command decision to make a break for it. Luckily the car was in the working mens' club the same as last year, so before the police really got to grips with the crowd we were in the car and edging through the throngs of people milling through the streets and we were gone. That was a lucky escape. People who were parked in the official car parks were trapped and their kit stranded. Those who were in that position either had to hang around in Liverpool for the weekend or make the journey back up for the one race when it was eventually run on the following Monday.

We used to work a lot of point to points back at that time. One bank holiday meeting resulted in us making the racing press. There was a big crowd but very few runners due to the fairly firm ground. One race only two were declared. Dave was at a loss how to try and stimulate some interest. There weren't many options open to him with several layers already betting on the distance. The forecast or straight was the only other option, apart from just not bothering, but with a big crowd just desperate to hand their money over there had to be a way. The forecast was the best bet he thought, so priced up one to beat the other and either horse to finish alone. Then at the last minute in a flash of inspiration he added 50/1 no finishers. That seemed to capture the imagination of the punters. They soon started having their pounds and two pound bets on. The serious punters were also betting the other options but still the small punters piled in. The column for the no finishers went right down the book and showed a loss of a monkey at the off. I had pointed out the mounting liabilities to the boss through the betting but he wasn't concerned. He had never known no finishers in all his bookmaking career and bear in mind these were the days when remounting was still allowed.

Of course, you don't have to be the lovechild offspring of Sherlock Holmes and Miss Marple to guess that as I have written that premise it all went horribly wrong for the intrepid bookie and the two runners. The first horse not to finish never even made it over the first fence but ran out ditching its jockey in the process and went careering into the woods and for the telling of this story was never seen again, at least for long enough. This left the long odds-on favourite to just jump around to claim the prize money bootie. That didn't go too well either; his jockey fell off two fences later. It was a very soft fall and the horse just sort of stood there so was caught by the fence official, which was handy as the jockey just had to hop back on and continue, except he couldn't. Soft fall or not he had injured himself and couldn't get back on. The boss had done his money in style, but the worst was yet to come. The announcer quite rightly declared the race void and informed punters that they were due their money back. That meant that not just the happy punters who were on at odds up to 50/1 were forming a cheerful queue for their winnings but also everyone else. This would have meant a much bigger disaster than it already was. The boss sprinted up to the commentary box, then another announcement was made that all bets were void except the bookie who offered the no finishers option. There were some disgruntled punters but the decision stood. The story even made the next day's racing press, a lucky escape in the end and an expensive lesson learned.

One point to point incident occurred when a well-backed horse won. The punters were paid out then it was subsequently disqualified. A lot of the punters who had backed the horse were familiar but un-named faces. One or two returned their winnings but most did a massive swerve around us when betting on the subsequent races. The boss was particularly incensed by one guy who had picked up a couple of hundred pounds, bet with us regularly but didn't return the money. He went on the missing list for the rest of the meeting and was either keeping a low profile or had missed the next few. Probably a month or so later the boss spotted our man and confronted him. He vehemently denied having ever been at the meeting let alone had the bet. What made the boss even angrier was that the guy seemed so belligerent in his denial even though it was definitely him. The final insult was his last retort that it could well have been his twin brother. The boss just gritted his teeth and made it clear that he didn't think much of his lack of honest sportsmanship and drew a line under the situation.

Quite often bookmakers' floor-staff were made up of retired ex bookies who were just looking to earn themselves a few extra quid and just keep involved with the game. After all, as I have found out, once in your blood it's in. The trouble with the old guard was, quite often they would have their own ideas about the game and were prone to have a little dispute with the 'young upstart' who was employing them for the day. That could be tolerated but the more serious problem came with the slowdown and deterioration of age that they were quite often in denial about. Deafness was the main one with just not being quite so 'with it' the other. New technology and grasping it was another, combine the two and there could be all sorts of fun and games. Just before I started on the new firm there was an incident at Salisbury that illustrated the fact quite well.

The boss had employed a lovely chap from Torquay who used to be a bookmaker a few years back. He had left the game and settled down to genteel retirement in the English Riviera playing bowls and generally enjoying himself. He liked to keep the odd day at the races so jumped at the chance for a summer's day out not too far away. The boss was always right up there with new ideas and had recently purchased some walkie-talkies. The idea was to send a man across the track to the silver ring where the market sometimes differed and value could be obtained. Dave could see what was going on around him in his location and hop off the stool to call bets in if need be or if there was better on offer on the other end of the radio he could hedge there. The other advantage was that the markets in the two rings differed slightly; given the nature of the punters in the 'cheap' side it was often harder for the books to get a short-priced favourite in the book. The result of this was that they would quite often go a fair bit bigger pricewise than in the main ring to entice the punters in.

On this particular day things were ticking along quite sedately until one race where there was a short-priced favourite. Dave wanted to oppose the horse and had it as his main lay of the day. Frustratingly for him once the betting got under way it became obvious that he wasn't the only one. The forecast price in the Sporting Life had been around 4/5 but already the horse was trading at a shade of odds against and not such value to lay.

As was his style he had been just making small books on the other races with not much in it profit-wise on the day. He needed to get this race right or it would have been a wasted journey. On the other hand there is a point where a horse is no longer value to lay. It seemed that others in the ring were determined to get the horse in the book and the danger was that they would chase the price out to a silly one. Suddenly there was hope on the horizon. The retired bookie floorman on the radio in the silver ring reported that the favourite was 4/6 out there. The boss questioned the price and was told that a mystery punter had come from nowhere and had a lump on so the modest books were running a bit scared.

Seeing his chance Dave told him to see if anyone wanted up to a £400 to £500. The radio went dead for a bit then it came back to life with the message 'Yes you have done that, in bits and pieces but the whole lot.' That was very handy indeed, while the rest of the ring were still fighting to get the horse in, the firm could sit back and relax, safe in the knowledge that the boss had laid the horse at the right price. He could easily have got stuck into the others and had a nice book but as the plan was to lay the horse and its weakness was a good sign all may not be right, the book was effectively closed.

As the race unfolded the favourite was soon in trouble and beaten well before the line. That was very handy, another plan came together and a profitable day ensured. The boss sent for ice-cream and was just about to radio over to invite his man in the other enclosure to buy himself one out of the winnings when to his surprise he turned up at the joint red-faced and flustered complaining about the trouble he had getting over due to the jobsworth on the gate. Dave told him with a smile he didn't need to bring the money over he could have waited until the last. That smile turned to horror when the reply was that as he had to beg for the bet there was no way that the bookies in question were going to wait for their monkey. He had backed the horse and not laid it, a turnaround of £900 which was huge. I am reliably informed that not one word was spoken in the journey back to Torquay. Needless to say, the ex-bookie stayed pretty much retired after that, his loss was my gain.

During that window of time from working with the previous firm and a year or so into the new one, was probably a golden time. At weekends we would be three handed but during the week it was quite often just Dave and I. The kit would be the gear, which consisted of a tripod, board, hod and field book. We would sometimes set off with the possibility of a few days away and the option of venues. Dave would take the bets and I'd stand next to him holding the field book and writing them down as we went. If a plan went right we might pack up and get some fish and chips before heading home or onwards or if it didn't we may do the same. It was a relaxed environment with a boss who didn't display too much emotion win or lose which meant working for him was a pleasure. Sometimes in the height of the summer we'd be at one venue and then decide to up sticks and head to an evening meeting instead.

We did get a bit of a shock at a point to point. We were just tapping away as normal when the boss tapped me on the arm and pointed with an astonished 'I can't believe it', identical twins, one of whom, though quite which one we'll never know, had a bet on a disqualified horse and never paid, and another who was wrongly accused. Well, we'll give him the benefit of the doubt as the boss did on the day.

Totally out of the blue one day early in 1998 Dave suggested to me that I become his representative on course. That was massive for me and I was over the moon. What it meant was that he was going to trust me to attend meetings on his behalf under his name and bet with his money even though he wasn't there. This really was a dream come true for me. It wouldn't be often but when a meeting clashed with a decent point he was going to send me racing. Points had different rules regarding reps so it wouldn't be the other way around. It was only just sinking in when he then added that I might as well jump in at the deep end and do the Grand National for my first outing.

So that's what happened. I managed to secure the services of an excellent clerk who had worked with Bevan and Lynn. He in turn was going to sort out a floorman. I met Dave on the Friday who gave me my instructions and the tank. Dave being Dave the instructions were basically, bet tidy if you can, do your best and don't be afraid to come home early if it is useless, oh, and that he really fancied Earth Summit so we had to keep that in the book for ourselves.

We set off bright and early, nervous but in eager anticipation at actually standing up as the bookmaker at the Grand National. Had anyone told me that as I was stood on guard in Germany a few short years ago I'd have been well-chuffed. We followed the same plan as before but left a lot earlier. As a result of the previous year's bomb scare it had been widely reported that security levels were going to be very high so everyone was told to expect delays due to searches of people and kit. We got there hours before the first so sailed through and just dumped our stuff waiting for pitch time. We weren't the first there but it was just as well we did get to the course early. As the morning went on the firms struggling to get in were getting more and more flustered at the 'anal' way they were being checked. Heaven forbid had it been in the computer era.

We had time to have a look around while things were being sorted out. They laid out the pitches. We were in a modest position in among many firms with which none of us were familiar. One northern operation next to us had set up a huge board offering a daily double featuring the National and the first race. It was around that time that Henry Rix was tipping in the Racing Post having been spotted picking a whole host of big-priced handicap winners in the Today newspaper. The non-national leg of the double was a race where he had tipped up Bellator. It was a fairly short price but that one coupled with Earth Summit was around 20/1. I had won a few quid following Henry in recent weeks so decided to chuck a fiver, no sod it, I'm the bookie today, a tenner at the double. The guy snatched my hand off, and that was that.

We got set up and ready to roll. I was a bit alarmed that John seemed to be giving his mate, who I had never met before, quite an in depth briefing, including writing down all the £100 to fractions on his card, something I used to do when learning.

I was more than a little concerned when John admitted that his mate had not only never done the job before but this was in fact the first time he had ever been to the races. Not much more than a little concerned though because we expected to do well and wouldn't be having many bets back, and not to get to the point that we were under the cosh business-wise. While the problem on the Embankment was frustrating that was nothing compared to the reports we heard from those trying to get into the main ring. The crowds were said to be bottle-necked at the checking points and backing up further and further up the access roads.

Our area seemed to be similarly populated to the last two years, busy but not all that busy, then all of a sudden it looked for all the world as if the crowd had burst through the barriers. There was a tsunami of people all heading our way. It transpired that as it was getting closer and closer to the first race the decision was made that all those queuing to get in who didn't have a ticket could go into the Embankment area for free, so in they poured. All of a sudden the ambiance had gone from a busy point to point to Cheltenham Gold Cup Day.

It was mayhem, punters clamouring to get on with bets

that it was hard for me to call accurately; luckily John was a trooper and did a sterling job of getting the bets down and dictating when a price needed to be shortened or lengthened. We were able to bet overs easily but it was all go; John's mate belied his green status and got to grips with paying out as we cracked on with the next race. Inexplicably Henry Rix's selection was a big drifter, not with us though, and won.

The National itself was madness. We kept Earth Summit short on our board but the punters kept backing it with us. John kept telling me to shorten it which I did but still they backed it with us, such was the scrum to get on. Had it been a normal day we would have taken all we could at the shorter odds and had it all back just before the off at bigger but it just wasn't possible. It was taking forever to pay winners from the last race and all we could do to keep up with the bets. They still kept backing Earth Summit amongst a whole host of others but in the end John told me to take it off the board all together. Punters who had battled to get to the joint were suddenly faced with no price. Of course they enquired what price it was. We told them truthfully, no price, but then lied through our teeth that we had taken so much money on the horse that if we took anymore and it won we would have to walk home, and we lived in Devon.

One or two punters grumbled and battled their way out to try and get on somewhere else but amazingly the majority sympathised with us and picked something else. By the off of the race we had Earth Summit winning a nice few quid. We may have had a couple of losers but a great book none the less. As the race unfolded it became more and more realistic that the dream result was on the cards, approaching the last a distinct possibility and on the run-in a reality. We screamed the horse home jumping like loons as it passed the post the winner. All around us other firms were cursing their luck as the winner was one of the well-fancied horses in the race.

It suddenly dawned on me that we may well have put a lot of half-cut racegoers off the winner, but a sheepish look around luckily didn't reveal an angry mob clutching losing tickets that should have been winning ones, itching to kill us.

Luckily for us it appeared that none of the people who had been told we'd have to walk home should the winner win were about to take their ire out on us. Once the dust had settled though it did seem that the firm next to us could well have been in the sort of dire financial straits where a bus ticket might well have come in handy. There was a right old shemozzle going on. The team, that seemed to consist of several interested parties were all having a pop at each other. One of them had fancied the winner, another had wanted to stand it, and then they all wanted to know whose stupid idea it was to offer the double. That reminded me, I had copped on that too but felt it prudent to hold on for a little while before going to draw, safe to say they were not happy and didn't pay out with a smile.

Not all of my outings as a representative went as well. One memorable occasion was at a point to point not too far from Tiverton. Reps were not normally allowed at points but if the pitch-holder was ill there was special dispensation. Dave was having an operation on his elbow so John and I were dispatched to the meeting clutching a letter to that effect. The meeting was memorable in the first instance because unusually it was being covered by the SIS (Satellite Information Services) as a trial run. It was a miserable cold and grey day with sporadic squally showers of sleet coming down to compound the misery. When it came to laying out the line the formidable Brian Edwards was in charge. He called the bookmaker's names in the order that their seniority commanded and one by one they took their positions and started to pitch up.

It appeared that quite a few of the other books there were aware that the boss was under the knife so expected a move up having no idea that I was now his official representative. Brian went through the motions and called out 'David Phillips.' He looked genuinely surprised when I called out yes, as did several of those whose names appeared further down the list. He huffed and puffed for a couple of seconds then barked that we couldn't bet. I protested that as the boss was ill I was entitled to bet. Brian, still huffing replied that I needed a letter from him to allow that to happen. There were some seriously put-out faces when I brandished the required document 'peace in our time' style. It was snatched from my hand, briefly examined and handed back in silence, the only acknowledgment that all was in order was the name of the next bookmaker's name being called.

The weather hadn't daunted the punters but it seemed to have an effect on the runners. Race after race threw up short-priced favourites. Our brief was to bet as tight as possible but once we had got the favourite in the book there was precious little money for anything else, so effectively you were just laying the favourites and hoping for the best. We did have the name of one horse to go for in the maiden should it run but we were there to lay the short-ones and at the prices we only needed to get one beaten to win on the day. They were jumping impeccably and winning with ease, in short we were doing the boss's money in cold blood.

One particular race featured a very short-priced favourite. We decided that we would get it in but because of the way things were going and the fact it looked a certainty we'd do it as short as possible. Looking around us the price was generally 1/6 with a few places going 2/11 and one at 1/5 so we joined in at 1/6. Unexpectedly a well-known 'face' came in with a bundle of readies, £1200 to win £200, which was perfect. We could have some back at 1/5 and sit back. I hopped off the stool and asked the layer next to me for a monkey at 1/5, it was still on his board. He looked at me through the tiny gap between his hat and thick scarf and shouted back a muffled

'Nothing' before replacing the price with a 1/7. I ran on down the line of frozen bookmakers none of whom were taking a bet looking to hedge, the 1/5 and 2/11 was all taken off before I could get close enough. Pure revenge we thought for having the audacity to turn up and bet depriving them of a move up.

We had no option but to stand the bet in its entirety. You are no doubt thinking that it wasn't really a bad bet to lay and we were only risking a couple of hundred quid. The trouble was we had no option but to lose around £100 or so every race so far and it was mounting up to a nice few quid. Points were supposed to be somewhere you went to try and nick yourself a day's wages not where you did a grand. Even losing that on a big racing day would be a bad one for our firm. John and I were desperate to impress but things were going horribly wrong. The only hope was that we would have the opportunity to crow like we'd never crowed before should the jolly hitch its foot or run out. It didn't, it totally hosed in.

Now we were in serious trouble. We had managed to take exactly £12 out of the rest of the field. The day was effectively already over but there was still the maiden and the chance of salvaging something and appeasing the boss a bit. Surprisingly compared to the other fields in the day there was a decent turnout for the maiden and even better our tip horse was running. Once we started betting we kept that one way shorter than everyone else and got stuck into the field. The betting was quite brisk being the only real betting race of the day. Punters who don't like to lump on the odds-on shots had kept their powder dry and were wading in. We were betting so well that we decided we were going to have a 'bar one' on our horse. We weren't betting that well that we didn't have a lot of losers in the book but we had fielded plenty. It wasn't classic or sensible bookmaking by any means but should our tip horse win, we'd not only get out on the day but would have covered the expenses and got the boss a few quid to boot.

The race was off and the worm had turned, our horse was jumping like a stag making the rest of the field look decidedly pedestrian. He sailed into a clear lead down the back straight and appeared to have put the rest to the sword. Flew towards the second last and fell. Disaster, the worst in the book went on to win and we had done our cobblers, or rather we had done Dave's cobblers. The news was hardly conducive to a speedy recovery from his operation and I have a feeling it was my last ever outing as his representative. In hindsight we had done it right, the horse that fell was Relaxation who went on to win the National Hunt Chase at Cheltenham.

# Chapter 8

*Frankie's Magnificent Seven And The New Era.*

It was at the end of that period that I was at Ascot to witness one of racing's most historic days, Frankie Dettori's magnificent seven winners. It would never have entered my head to get involved with backing all of his mounts but I do remember very clearly Derek Thompson interviewing the jockey before racing. They were stood on a little podium in front of the stands. I remember making a sub-conscious note that he had given all his mounts a fair chance. That thought was it, not 'nearly' backing them all. That was a mug bet, and of course we were far too professional a firm to get involved with those type of bookie-friendly mug bets. We were betting at the 'wrong' end of the betting ring but the meeting was a busy one by our standards and kept us on our toes. It wasn't unusual for a top jockey to ride a double or maybe even a treble in a day but what happened on that day was unprecedented.

It has been well-documented the way the results unfolded so I won't turn this into a history lesson that everyone knows but by the last race the whole course was abuzz. Although it was Frankie who had ridden all of the previous winners and that made it exceptional, if you had seen the results just laid bare in relation to SPs they were not exceptional with the biggest price being 12/1. The last race was a very competitive handicap, the general consensus of opinion being that although it would be lovely in reality it was unlikely that Frankie would bag all seven. I don't have any tales of telephone number sized bets that the boss took knowing that he couldn't pay as others have regaled us with. He did realise what was going to happen as far as the off-course firms though, so was up early at 3/1 in the hope that some 'mug' might take it off him. The ink wasn't dry on the board when he was asked for and laid a monkey at that price. That is what he stood Fujiyama Crest for and roared it home as did much of the ring around us.

It was around this time that I started getting writing ambitions in the racing world. I started to cover the local meetings for the Tiverton Gazette and got an actual paid column in a sort of racing fanzine called Final Furlong. The latter didn't last long but my Gazette reports continued on and off for a decade. My writing experience thus far had been writing about music in fanzines which I continued to do in parallel to my racing adventures.

Dave always was one to try new things out. One of the things he adopted which as it turned out was really prophetic was betting to numbers not horses. Traditionally when the bookmaker called a bet to the clerk it would be the horse's name. This was OK in small fields but in big handicaps slowed things down considerably. Clerks usually wrote the horses in the book in betting order so trying to find the correct column for horses that there had been an unexpected flow of money for, was slow. Usually as the boss was already rattling off the next bet he decided very logically to call the race card number. That way the clerk was right on the correct column and it also ruled out disputes where there were horses of a similar name.

The bookmakers were generally very traditional and even this little innovation was scoffed at in some quarters despite being totally logical and very effective. Unknown to us as the time it was also very good practise for the forthcoming computer age on the racecourse.

The idea for computerisation had been popping its head above the parapet for a while with the popularity of home computing growing. Eventually the bookies decided to at least investigate the possibility of bringing the on-course operation into the 20<sup>th</sup> century just as the 21<sup>st</sup> loomed. Apparently the Australians had been using computerised systems for some time, so a delegate was chosen to fly over to investigate. Respected Welsh layer John Lovell was dispatched to go and check out the viability of adopting the system in the UK. Despite this move it still seemed at the time that most of the bookmaking fraternity were hoping that he'd come back saying that it may have been OK in the Aussie sunshine but wouldn't be practical in Exeter's horizontal rain.

On his return his enthusiasm was met with incredulous dismissal in most quarters but John appeared determined to keep swimming against the tide. The sight of the Lovell firm struggling into the racecourses of the west with all their gear attracted a lot of attention and curiosity as well as downright ridicule. For starters the kit was very cumbersome because it needed a car battery to run, but in reality two because one wouldn't last long enough for a whole meeting. The kit itself was a laptop, keyboard and printer with all the wires that linked it all together. The only equipment available to aid in supporting the technology were the piles of possibly pre-war boxes made from old beer crates.

So there they would be, John looking a touch baffled. He had done the research but had limited technical knowledge, watching over his man who did know how it all worked. Their pitch looked like Pippin's Fort. They needed so many boxes, the printer balancing precariously on a teetering 'Jenga' of them with another construction supporting the contraption holding the laptop. After all it was only designed for a field book. These were relatively early days of the former too.

The difference between the old system and the new was huge. The 1800s quantum leaped into virtually the 21<sup>st</sup> century. Instead of a field book and a pencil with the bookmaker dishing out cards there was a computer and a printer. The bookie would call the bet, by race card number not name, which was the first change from tradition (unless you count my boss, Dave). The clerk would tap in the bet on the keyboard and out would come a ticket. The ticket would contain all the information a punter needed, the name of the horse they had backed, how much they had staked, their potential return and the name of the bookmaker. This was an obvious benefit to punters, especially those on big days and weekends when they were not so familiar with how the on-course system worked.

Although the system of the field book and cards that had been in place for over a hundred years was tried and tested it was open to problems, mainly human error, or nature. Many times in the past we were asked how the bookie knew what bet they had just by giving them a bit of card. Even when it was explained some people seemed dubious. After all they had just left their hard-earned money with, if the TV pundits' hyperbole was to be believed, a dastardly bookmaker. Of course very few bookmakers were dastardly, far less than the punters, but unintentional mistakes just down to human error often reinforced that opinion.

Occasional mistakes by the clerk resulted in a bet being placed under the wrong horse in the field book or the each-way part being omitted, even the stake incorrectly entered. There was nothing a bookie needed less than a dispute. More often than not when a ticket was brought up and initially rejected by the clerk the discrepancy would soon be rectified. The clerk would spot an obvious mistake or the bookmaker would remember the bet. Of course, the punter thought that we had been the victim of a potential stroke by the layers and went off telling all, who would listen, that so and so was crooked.

More likely however was the scenario where the punter actually asked for the wrong horse, meant to ask for each-way but didn't, was slightly worse for wear for drink or just plain trying it on. To combat this most bookmakers had a tape recorder in the hod, usually the small Dictaphone type, which would hopefully pick up what had been said when the bet was struck and settle the argument with genuine mistakes. The devious would hopefully be put off too. The trouble was though, any dispute regardless of if it had been the bookmaker's fault or not was time consuming, hassle, and kept at least one member of staff away from his job.

The new system came into its own in that respect. It was still possible for a mistake to be made, but if a punter came back a minute or so later complaining that they had asked and paid for an each way bet but only been given a win bet the error could be rectified before the race was run. The punter would still go away grumbling thinking that those dastardly bookies had tried to have him over again, but also in the warm glow that he had spotted it and scuppered their plan, probably with a spring in his step. The same went for betting the wrong horse. With the computer system the punters were encouraged to call the horse's number not the name. One of the most common mistakes would be they would call the horses' odds they wanted to back rather than the race card number.

The race card numbers were above the name on the list in the bookmaker's board but the odds right next to the name. For singular odds like 3/1 most bookies would just write 3. Sometimes it would be easy to spot when someone came in and asked for the odds rather than the number but if it wasn't they'd usually march up and say that the bookie had made a mistake. That was OK, because it was before the race.

It also made it a whole lot easier for the firm themselves to spot their own mistakes. The boss would check each ticket and make sure it was the same as the bet he had just called. If it was OK he would pass the receipt on to the punter or if not give the clerk a bollocking and get him to correct it. The other massive bonus was the speed and accuracy of paying out. Traditionally, when a punter came back with a ticket, the boss would call the last two numbers of the three on the ticket, the clerk would check his ledger and tell the boss what was to come. If the betting for the next race was well under way that would mean the clerk had to stop taking bets and verify the pay-out.

On really busy days like festivals there would be several books used and late bets written down on separate pieces of paper but some run of the mill days turned busy unexpectedly so speed of payment was essential. Accuracy also. A lot of punters thought that they had the right to call the bookmaker all the obscenities under the sun should they make an error that was costly to them. With weird logic if it was the other way around a lot of them considered you fair game. One example, before computers, was at a Cheltenham off meeting where we bet down by the paddock. It was unusually busy, blowy and wet. We were huddled under the arch that leads to the lower area of Tattersalls. Dave had gone wandering while his son and I paid out. We had taken a couple of hundred bets.

The book was like mush and we were freezing when a well-dressed guy came up to us with a soggy ticket and apologised, in a cut-glass accent, for bothering us with such a trifling sum. The boss's son called over to ask me what ticket it was that was due, using the last two digits. I looked down through the book and thought how the other half live. The 'trifling' was £165. In hindsight we should have checked again but he took the money without question and scampered off at double quick time. We thought nothing of it until a little while later a punter came over with a ticket. This time he gave the ticket direct to me, so I checked all three numbers. To my horror we had paid his ticket already, £165. Of course we had to pay him what he was owed. It was his bet regardless of the ticket. The boss wasn't best pleased though, the first guy we paid had only £3 to come!

There was always a huddle around the sometimes chaotic Lovell team or odd new firm trying the kit out. It mainly consisted of scoffing clerks and bookmakers nudging each other as the team struggled to get to grips with all the new equipment. The last time there had been such apparent desire to see a new innovation fail was when Stephen Little, the mink clad layer of monumental sums, tried to introduce South African style boards with little knobs that had to be turned to change prices. There had been much mirth at his expense as he struggled to get to grips with the device. He did persevere for a while but eventually accepted that it wasn't going to catch on.

The computer was something that Dave could see the potential in, not least for the reasons laid out above. Even if it was going to be a bit slower than the clerks, though that argument was more bluster than fact, maybe. The benefits would outweigh the problems. It wasn't long before we were trying out the kit for a day's racing. At that time there was only the one bit of active kit with just John's guy who seemed to know how to put it all together and work it. So that was the deal, we turned up and John's guy Lawrence was tasked to put everything together and then work as the clerk on the computer. It was a thankless task for him, forever with an audience, at the mercy of the apparently cantankerous computer and a bookmaker rattling bets off too quickly. Our trial day was riddled with minor problems but at the end of it John Lovell had a sale. We were heading into the computer age.

The plan was that we would borrow Lawrence for a few meetings while the rest of us learned how to work the system on the job. That idea worked well for a meeting or so then it was time for us to set out on our own, with the understanding that Lawrence would be there should we have any problems. That was an idea great in theory but there was a flourishing interest in at least trying the kit and only one of him. We had a rough idea of what to do so Dave decided on a quiet midweek meeting at Bath to unleash ourselves on the betting world. It was all a bit of a shambles. We couldn't get the kit set up

113

properly. There was no help available.

By the time we did have everything up and working there were only a few minutes left before the race. We priced up with the favourite at even money. The trouble was we had been so preoccupied with getting the kit set up nobody had noticed that the price of the jolly had collapsed. As soon as we went live a cash punter came in with an even monkey, the relative buttons were pressed, then a grinding sound as the ticket jammed in the printer. The punter was assured that he was on and given an old-style card simultaneously as it dawned on us that the horse's price was 4/6. There was nothing we could do apart from sit back and sweat. A one horse book with that one horse losing a monkey wasn't really the boss's style but it was our lucky day, we got away with it, the horse was beaten. That was enough for Dave. We had got the expenses out of pure luck. We packed up and headed home after just one race.

The next day was spent in his garage down in Torquay. The kit was set up and we took it down again, then set it up and again, repeated. Once we were satisfied that we'd pretty much got the set-up we then learned out how to work using the system, calling in bets, having hedge bets, and checking each ticket as they came out before handing them to the punters. There were already rumblings that once you handed a punter a ticket you had to honour it, even if you'd given them the wrong odds or typed in a £1000 bet instead of a tenner. There had been no precedent set at that early stage but we didn't want to be the ones to set it. An extra set of everything apart from the actual computer was bought too. We were now probably the most clued up team using a computer on the track, though to be fair there wasn't a lot of competition.

One of the main problems in those early days was power. The lightweight batteries we are used to these days hadn't been invented. The only real option available to us was to use car batteries. These were very heavy and spilled acid and we needed two to be on the safe side to last for a meeting. Days when we used to have to just bring in a joint and a hod were longed for as we struggled into racecourses with these batteries. We tried various methods of transportation. Shopping baskets favoured by old ladies were tried but the wheels designed to support some groceries and little more soon buckled under the weight. Wheeled suitcases fared slightly better but suffered a similar fate. Nobody really ever came up with a universally adopted system but we were always on the lookout for a good idea to poach.

First job for the boss when he got home was to stick the batteries on charge. That was OK when it was in his own garage but the fun and games started when we were doing stints away. That is why it was a good idea to try and hide the fact you had a couple of car batteries on you when you checked into a hotel or even worse a bed and breakfast. The bubble and fizz of the charging process wasn't really an aid to restful sleep, and of course, charging duties were down to the staff.

There were lots of hiccups and system faults not to mention upgrades in those early days, but we did realise very soon that the tickets were a hit with the punters. Saying that, the old-school moaned like hell but they could go down to a name just the same so that didn't really matter. Weekends were the times when many more first time or relative novices came racing. They had a built in mistrust of bookmakers, often fuelled and perpetuated by traditional ideas that they had, the loud-mouthed braggadocio who would do anything to steal and cheat you of your money at the earliest opportunity. That caricature was of course totally false, at least the last bit. Very few bookies would actually try and cheat or steal from you. There were one or two who would try and skim a few quid by rounding down each way payments etc but they were frowned upon by the majority of layers in the ring. Most were trying to shake off the old image.

We were that new-look bookie, young and smart with computerised tickets. In fact we had signs made up advertising the fact that we were issuing them. The punters loved them but that went over the heads of a lot of the other bookmakers who couldn't wait to have a laugh at your expense when the system threw up a glitch, your battery ran out of juice or your printer jammed. They didn't realise that when everything was working properly we were all over them.

At least at first, it didn't take long for the penny to drop. The first year we used the system at the Cheltenham Festival a few eyebrows were raised that we had risked using that gremlin-ridden kit on what was our big payday meeting of the year. Our next door neighbours were the firm I had started out with, Jack Lynn. They were like a well-oiled machine as usual, two clerks, a separate pay-out at the back of the joint and loads of sharpened pencils. We too were prepared. The pay-outs were well-rehearsed as the boss called the bet the person next to him took the ticket as it was spat out and checked it before handing it to the punter. The logic being that if we were certain that we had given out the correct ticket we could just pay out what it said on the winning ones. We did get a printout that we could check serial numbers off on, but to make things quicker we decided to partially rip the tickets and pay them before depositing them into a separate envelope for each race. There were one or two computer freeze-up incidents and the odd jammed ticket, but the Tuesday went very well.

Next door had been keeping an eye on us all day without saying anything but after the last race Roy couldn't help but to come and ask how things went. The boss was well aware that we had adopted something that had given us a real edge. Not just with the paying out either. The computer told you exactly where you were with the field money and take outs at all times. The best clerk, even those doubled up like next door couldn't keep up with all the bets, take outs and field money when things were very busy. And of course, no clerk is fail-proof under pressure. As long as we were happy that the correct ticket had gone out for each bet and we were, we were always on top of the game. With this in mind, he played down how well it had gone and mentioned the odd problem we had and also divided the turnover figure knowing for a fact that it would be well below what the well-organised bookie next door had managed to turn over. He seemed quite happy with that and probably went back to report that we had done it all wrong.

The next day all went well with the journey until we unpacked the kit. No printer. There was a brief round-robin of blame while the Torquay contingent all pointed the finger at each other for not packing it. I couldn't work out why it was ever taken out of the car but wasn't going to chip in. I decided to let them get on with it and go for a wander, but just as I almost got out of earshot I heard my name being hollered. It couldn't be my fault could it, even in the all-encompassing rule that the buck stopped with the floor man. By this point the ruck had resulted in the clerk, Adge, chain-smoking and next door taking a great deal of interest in what was being argued about. After all, why were we so bothered when the computer had been a bit slow and we only took a fraction of what they had?

Dave took me to one side away from prying ears and asked me to go back to the car and drive back to get the printer. I replied a bit incredulously, that was getting on for a six hour round trip. He reassured me that his Mrs was already on her way and was going to meet me at Taunton services. So off I went, discreetly, as I had been told. It wasn't easy trying to go against the flow of traffic trying to get into the festival, but eventually managed it and was told to not spare the horsepower getting to Taunton. By the time I arrived it was still half an hour before the first race. I collected the missing item from his flustered and quite put out Mrs and headed back from whence I came not holding the horses. I quite liked that order.

Betting was well under way for the third by the time I got back. It was busy, after all I wasn't there. Dave was pleasantly surprised how quickly I had made it back, but the computer kit was all set up ready to go, just needing the printer to be plugged in. As I handed the previously AWOL item over I caught the entire team next door gazing at us in disbelief. The secret was out. They knew that there was no way that the boss would have sent me all the way back to, as far as they knew Torquay, to get a printer unless using the system was a huge advantage over a field book. Roy Lynn next door lingered a bit longer. You just knew by the look on his face that he realised that he had been put away. Nothing more was said at that meeting but the very next week Lawrence was on duty showing them the ropes trialling the computer system.

It took quite some time, which was good for us, for people to catch on with the computers. For the outsider they didn't look too attractive a proposition. Everyone could see our trials and tribulations as we struggled in with all those car batteries and had a laugh at the weird and wonderful experimentation with transporting it. I ruined at least two suits by spilling acid on them. There was little sympathy if we arrived late and there were few boxes left. After all most firms needed four at the most, we were after piles of them. Anyone with any design and metalworking skills in the Torquay area was soon in demand trying to fabricate bits of metal to hold laptops and printers.

It wasn't just other bookmakers and punters who had started to notice the pioneering layers but journalists too. Dave Phillips was mentioned by name in the Racing Post after a writer overheard a couple of racegoers talking to each other about how they were choosing to bet with us rather than any other bookies because they could see what bet they had and how much they had to come back. He wrote a little piece on the new system and the benefits of it for punters. We wanted the punters to be happy, that goes without saying, but it was the benefit to us that really kept us pushing on. There were still plenty of glitches. The system could not be described as reliable because if you went a whole meeting without at least one problem it was considered a result. Computer systems were still quite basic and definitely not designed for use outdoors and bumped and bashed as ours tended to be.

The slow pace at which other layers were picking up on our advantage is illustrated by the fact that the next real eureka moment for another bookie was the height of summer. We were betting in our preferred position on the grass at the 'wrong' end of the front row at Glorious Goodwood. It was a baking hot day and we were betting tidily taking on the small punters. That was just the game of the bookmaker betting next to us. The difference was that we literally had a queue pretty much all afternoon. The guy next door could not understand it. He kept shouting to his floorman to 'keep him out' getting more and more flustered. His man responded quite correctly telling him that he 'was out.' The scene got more humorous as the day went on, the man on the stool got redder and redder as his floor man got angrier and angrier. The bookie then started hopping off his stool himself looking with pursed lips at our prices, then his then back again, they were the same, soon some of his were better, still they bet with us. The very next meeting, Lawrence was in action again.

We always realised that our advantage with computers was only going to last a while. As with anything in bookmaking, if you found an edge you had to run with it while you could because it was certain that it wouldn't be long before others caught up. As we had been there from the start we also had our fair share of disasters in the early days but reaped the rewards once the system and our skills with it improved. It was a little galling to see others watch and monitor from the sidelines then jump in to the computer age when the going was good, but that was life.

# Chapter 9

*If It's Not Broke, Don't Fix It.*

One problem with the proliferation of computers was everyone needed four or five times as many boxes on which to stack up to use their kit. There were humorous scenes as early birds built themselves veritable forts. This caused several rows as the habitually late had to call in favours to get enough to work with, in many cases soon finding out who their friends really were. That problem was soon to be solved by regulation from an organisation that nobody wanted. The NJPC.

The National Joint Pitch Council was a body set up to take over administration from the bookmakers themselves. There had been rumblings for a while that the closed shop, dead man's shoes system of allocating pitches was an unfair one, which of course it was. It wasn't surprising that those already incumbent in the betting ring didn't really want things to change but the system had no place in the modern world. For some time bookmakers had been complaining that despite having a licence and money they were not allowed to bet on busy days despite books being thin on the ground due to clashes of meetings. The first appeasement was the introduction of the aforementioned extended supplementary list, with the disastrous results to the ring already related.

The clamour to bet and the obvious belief that the pot of gold at the end of the rainbow was in the betting ring was frantic. Those who had been scraping in at the bottom of the list and finding it costly weren't put off by the bloody noses dished out by the punters. They could see men of advancing years in the front rows pottering away, in the opinion of the green-eyed monsters in the back row, 'flimping' the punters and not really working a pitch that they could work so much better. Once again racecourses had their ears bashed; there were people out there with money who would happily pay to bet in those better positions. On the other hand, the bookmakers didn't own anything but the right to bet in certain spots. A right sometimes inherited over generations.

Many hadn't amassed the riches that people watching their posteriors day in day out assumed they had. They could do without the freezing wet wintery weather but had to keep working to keep their pitch, and in many cases to keep the wolf from the door. The idea that they could sell their pitch was very attractive to a lot of them. It was not only bookies betting in poor pitches who were going to be keen to upgrade but also those on waiting lists who had rarely bet on course and some who had no experience at all and just fancied becoming a bookie.

# Chapter 10

*Buying And Selling Pitches.*

It was eventually agreed that bookmakers would be able to buy and sell their pitches. The NJPC was set up to administrate the rings and the auctions. It was the biggest shake-up the betting rings of the UK had ever seen.

Auctions were hugely anticipated and well-attended, the ring was never to be the same again. The meetings after the first of these took place were unrecognisable in places, at least in the betting ring. Quite a few of the old-school who had held front-row pitches for years but were more than happy to tread water sold up and retired to places like Brighton. Many of these positions were snapped up by existing layers who knew the value of those positions but there were also some totally new faces who spent a lot of money. A few of these firms were established bookmakers from dog track and point to point backgrounds but some were green as grass, and were there for picking off.

Some of these new guys had hired seasoned racecourse regulars to run the pitches for them. Those floormen and clerks, on a nifty or so a day, were soon being regaled with tales of people suddenly elevated to riches, company cars, three figure sums a day, bonus schemes, and a whole lot more besides. Those on more modest remuneration accepted their pay because they also knew exactly how well their paymaster had done to the penny day to day. Eyebrows were raised wondering how people betting in the pitches we had probably all bet in from time to time, were going to finance all these riches.

Eyebrows were raised again (we could have done with

Patrick Moore in the ring at the time, there was so much eyebrow raising going on) at some of the people who had appeared to have persuaded people with money to let them run their business. Some of the new investors were going to be present whilst others seemed content to sit at home and wait for the cash cow they had just invested in to deliver the goods. It's not that the people involved were dishonest, but more often than not totally inexperienced at the level they were now attempting to be at.

Lower down the list of pitches sold there had obviously been very little research done into their viability. There were cases of people selling pitches so poor that they rarely worked them, going for figures way above what they were worth, while better ones, later on in the auction were going unsold. At the other end of the scale some of the top pitches in the country were going for figures that made the eyes water. They were also to make high-rolling clever punters mouths do the same when they read of new pitch holders talking of looking forward to doing battle with all-comers.

Bookies were quite often targets for people trying it on, but unless they were being careless, rarely succumbed. The reason for this was they had served their apprenticeship and were wise to pretty much every trick that people tried to use. From simple things like people giving you a tenner, then after they watched you throw it in the bag claim it was a score, to calling ambiguous bets to people, earwigging bets called then sending a 'moody' floorman in to claim a bet called down to a firm before the real floorman came in to draw. Those sorts of stories were soon flying around the racecourses of the country; nobody was keen to admit that they were true of course. Some staff holding long-standing jobs with established firms were lured by promises of riches. They had spent years watching the money roll in. Most were well-rewarded but a mixture of greed and ambition led to the smell of burning bridges mingling with

124

the musty aroma of bad breakups in the betting ring.

Other sales were by bookmakers who had attained fair positions at places they didn't really want but took because they had been allocated after a long wait. They were being snapped up by people who didn't stop to ask themselves why they were being sold. A lot were OK but the owners wanted to move up so maybe sold four bad pitches to buy one good one at their local tracks. Others were an expensive lesson to their new owners. It wasn't long before a whole new business started within the buying and selling market. Maverick high-rolling bookmaker Stephen Little was soon a regular sight walking around the ring in his vintage mink coat selling his home-printed 'Pitchform' lists for a tenner a pop, listing the latest sales and transactions.

Predictably there were very expensive lessons learned very quickly. Some firms who had made the early headlines with their huge investments made them again being the first to discover that the betting ring was not paved in gold. Their failure was for a variety of reasons, mainly experience. Some of the people who had talked the good talk and wormed their way into jobs as mentors were indeed established bookies but had little knowledge of the level at which the new firms were pitching in. Very shrewd operators who had given up trying to get bets on, at the right prices on-course, were back. They were highly delighted to find new firms who would take whatever bets they wanted to offer them, briefly of course. Those who thought all they had to do was fill the bag with money and the results would look after themselves soon learned that it didn't quite work like that. It was quite a sad sight to see, when new firms, run by very nice people, started to turn up on courses betting in fairly poor positions being picked off.

People who only had previous experience as floormen soon had to get used to the uncomfortable experience of explaining meeting after meeting, why they had not only not won but once again lost the tank. It was only a matter of weeks before the first of the high-profile new firms had exited the market with their tails between their legs leaving a whole lot of money behind in the betting ring and some newly redundant staff eating huge portions of humble pie in the hope of getting work again.

On the plus side, old boys with no family who had worked hard all of their lives in the betting ring got to retire with enough money to make their twilight years comfortable. At the same time, when the dust settled and the mayfly firms had burned brightly then bowed out, established layers who were going to work those good pitches to their full potential got to do so.

The problem for the rest of the ring was that once again it was just like the days a few years prior to the ESL. Full betting rings on quiet days, layers with deep pockets in the front rows trying to take every penny and more Indians queuing up to take the place of those who fell by the wayside. On the plus side, the sharp ones were getting some great value backing live ones and silly amounts of money for pitches that had really been pretty worthless to them.

The NJPC started running the betting ring, taking over from the self-regulated way it had been done for decades. Little changed in that respect but there were soon rows when the system of 'seniority' was brought into play. New bookies who had bought pitches were becoming incensed when they were leapfrogged for move ups by long-standing layers who were behind them. The loudest mouths quite often get heard better in bookmaking and this was no exception. It has to be said they had a valid argument which they won in the end.

The next thing that the NJPC wanted to do was bring uniformity into the ring. That was a huge call in an environment that was made up of and thrived on diversity. Their method for doing this was not uniforms as some wags had suggested but new joints that looked the same. These were sturdy and designed to hold computers and printers, and had a built in hod. They also cost a nice few quid and added to the already growing amount of kit being dragged onto the racecourse every day. There was only one type of joint on offer to bookmakers at first, a really solid sturdy effort that was very robust but heavy. It came in two plastic boxes on wheels. There was soon a competitor, a much more lightweight version made in a similar way to a child's Wendy house with tubes and material to cover it. These were a much cheaper option and initially very popular so immediately the idea of uniformity was out of the window, especially when bookmakers could use their own headboards.

The ensuing few weeks after the new joints were in and the tripods were out were great comedy value. It didn't help with the timing of their delivery. Ours and several others were delivered on Derby Day at Epsom of all days. Typical of my boss ours just stayed in their two canvas suitcases but other firms were super keen to get theirs out and up. Instructions were out and staff set about the construction of the new purchase while bosses generally stood and directed affairs with as much positive effect as a blind man directing traffic.

Tempers were frayed then lost completely as the deceptively simple way these things were set up, as displayed by the fellow that sold them, proved tricky. Weird and wonderful shapes were thrown care of oddly attached poles while heads were scratched looking at extra ones. The chaos that ensued before racing was nothing compared to that after. Layers used to getting out of racecourses as quickly as possible after racing, especially at meetings like the Derby, were exasperated as their staff, and for the more hands-on, they themselves attempted to get all those panels of plastic, canvas and confounded poles back into their suitcases. Some firms resorted to just bundling it all up in their arms and struggling out of the course like many an inept camper cursing as they went. As per the new computer we took time out to get used to unpacking and packing the kit, which in actual fact wasn't all that complicated when you had time to do it methodically.

The other joints were more like Meccano and in time proved to be the better investment, as they were easier to erect in bad weather and then keep earth-bound. Several of those original joints (there have been several upgrades over the years) can still be seen on the racecourse. I have seen an old Wendy house joint from time to time in far-flung silver rings on a busy bank holiday, but they generally didn't make it to the millennium celebrations and there was never an upgrade.

The NJPC seemed to have money coming out of their ears back in those days. I was tempted to apply for one of the jobs that they created. People were employed to travel around racecourses with a small articulated trailer attached to a van. The idea was to travel from track to track as part of the travelling circus that is racing as a provider of information to novice punters. What a job that looked to be. Drive the van to the course, set it all up and sit there chatting to punters. The pay wasn't bad either but the usefulness and 'money well spent' ideal of it was in question. There was maybe justification for these information areas on Bank Holidays, Saturdays and festival meetings, but on a wet Tuesday in February at the top of Haldon Hill where Exeter racecourse sits, only generally hardened and experienced racegoers brave the horizontal rain so the NJPC trailers only use was to shelter from it.

Those vehicles and the jobs for the people driving and manning them didn't last too long. After the initial euphoria and influx of money it soon became apparent to people who thought the pot of gold lay at the end of the back line at Goodwood on a wet weekday, that this was not the case. The trouble was like the 'Indians' before when the ESL first came into existence there seemed to be a never-ending succession of

128

bookmakers who, because they had bought their pitches and could only sell them at a massive loss kept coming out to give it another go. Places that would normally have been bettable on an off day because of a clash in meetings were still getting far too many bookies for the punters in attendance.

After one particularly bad afternoon at Epsom where everything that could go wrong did go wrong Dave spent the very silent journey home ominously crossing out meetings in his diary. When we got to my drop off point he broke it to me that he was going to have to start cutting down on the days we were attending. It was only going to be the local tracks and the good meetings. This was a real blow as it was my only source of income unless we managed to back a winner. To ease the blow he took us all on a timeshare holiday to Portugal for a week. That was late September. To be fair we pottered around going to a few more meetings than he had originally said. I got a few odd days with other bookies but it was almost impossible to survive. I worked Cheltenham 2000 and the next day took off on a plane bound for Singapore after selling everything I owned, which was not a lot, and armed myself with a couple of credit cards. The day after cheering home Looks Like Trouble in the Gold Cup I was sweating it out watching flood-lit flat racing at Kranji.

# Chapter 11

*Around The World In Many Days.*

My adventures included as mentioned racing at Kranji, Bangkok Turf Club in Thailand and the Melbourne Cup at Flemington. I backed Martin Pipe's Far Cry. He was over in Australia for a week beforehand. It had to be an omen. The commentator gave it every chance before it broke down. The race was won by an outsider called The Brew. The race was sponsored by Fosters Lager. It had to be a certainty one well-dressed but quite refreshed Aussie guy, told me. In hindsight I suppose it was, but as he was wearing a VB box on his head I didn't take too much notice.

My year travelling the world came to an end around the 1st of February 2001 when the cash machine on Koh Samui Thailand finally stopped giving me cash advances from my credit card, long after my cash ran out. I had been living in a beach hut on the island since Christmas and had become very much at home living as a beach bum, eating local food and swimming the waters of the bath-warm bay every morning. Reality had to be faced, I had told myself that as soon as the money ran out I would head for home. I didn't want to the be at the stage where I was down to my last couple of quid and living on rice before getting back. After almost a year of travelling I knew to expect the unexpected, especially in Thailand. I said my goodbyes to all the Thai people with whom I had become friendly with over the last couple of months, the UK ex-pats and the island itself and headed back to Tiverton.

The shock was tantamount to cruel. Within two days of the machine letting me know that I had insufficient funds I was in Bangkok for one last hurrah on Koh San Road and before the Singah and Sang Som fuelled hangover had a chance to abate I was on a Qantas flight back to the UK. God bless that airline. I told a hostess in economy I was depressed after spending almost a year away including a wonderful six months in her country. I was heading back to, as my newly found on the first day in Australia mate 'Aussie' Nick put it, 'Dreary old Pommyland.' By the look on her face I could tell she emphatically felt my pain. I asked if she could help me out with an extra drink or two to ease the misery. That wonderful girl ensured my plastic wine glass was never empty until I was safely asleep.

I remember very little of my journey home from the airport, not because of drink but probably because I was in complete denial. One weird thing was that I had a recurring dream when I was away that I had fallen asleep on a bus in whatever country I was in (I did a lot of bus miles) and had woken up to find, to my horror, that I was at the Tiverton turn off at junction 27 on the M5. For that reason alone I took the much more expensive train back home. I sat for two hours quietly with my thoughts gazing unseeing out of the rain thrashed window wistfully wondering if the last year had been just a dream. I was conscious that we had passed Taunton so only had around 15 minutes left but was in no hurry to extricate myself from my comfortable cocoon of misery. Then it hit me, like one of those old 1950's horror films where the shocking bit is accentuated by a rapid zoom in zoom out moment accompanied by a sudden blast of over the top music.

You could bloody well see that sign, the blue one that haunted so many dreams in places like Sydney, Chang Mai and The Perhentian Islands, from the bloody train. It was like an alarm clock had gone off in my head, the dream year was over, I was at Tiverton Parkway and it was pissing down with rain.

After realising during the foot and mouth demolition of

131

racing that I was in fact qualified to do nothing apart from racing, and suffering that barren period screwing on bottle tops in a perfume factory for the minimum wage, I had to up my game. I got some cards made up using the local night club's photocopier and laminate machine and planned to distribute them around the racecourses hoping to pick up the odd day's work while fully expecting to keep working mainly for Dave Phillips.

# Chapter 12

*Dorset Farmer To The Rescue.*

The first day I dished them out was at Chepstow and I got a bite just down the line. Ivor Perry and Co was owned by wealthy farmer and racehorse owner of the same name. He had a reputation for laying some of the bigger bets on course as well as being a shrewd firm. The old man had recently retired and handed the business over to his daughter Wendy and soon to be son-in-law Jo. They had a guy who was a family friend already helping them but had suffered some disasters due to his inexperience. It would be churlish to go into them but punters of an unscrupulous nature can sniff those sorts of people out from a long way out and pounce at the earliest opportunity, a costly business when you take bets in thousands. The firm raced very regularly too, I was going to earn a decent living given the amount of meetings they bet at a year. Add to that the bonuses that were promised as well as inspired inside info it had me thinking I had reached the Promised Land that I had always aspired to since that first day I started with Jack Lynn.

Actually I will tell you because I am going to edit all the names out of this so nobody is going to get upset. On one occasion they had laid a winning bet of a grand at five to two. The fella who had the bet was the only one left to draw so the family friend was asked to wait on the joint to pay the three and a half grand when he resurfaced. The daughter and son-in-law were off to the paddock as was their usual routine. This was essential as they were excellent form judges. When they returned the guy was stood on the stool but ashen-faced. He had paid the bet OK, all of it, three and a half grand in cash.

What was the problem then? The guy had given him a losing ticket and was still in possession of the winning one.

This was a disaster; in the earlier days of computers the punters were pretty much always given the benefit of the doubt. If the guy reappeared with the ticket at a later date, even though he had blatantly been paid it was almost certain that he would be offered half. The only option was to try and find the guy. He was quite distinctive and known to some of the bookies, and unfortunately as one you always had to check the bundles of when he had a bet, which didn't auger well. The racecourse was searched high and low. Luckily Ivor scoured the parts of the racecourse less travelled and spotted the guy. He collared him, almost literally. Those big farmer's hands weren't going to let go once he'd got his man. Rather flustered the guy said the ticket was in his car, pretty much proof that he was up to no good, and that he would pop out and get it. Yes he would but only aided out there by the same vice-like grip. The ticket was returned and the guy courteously thanked even though everyone knew he was certainly going to try it at a later date. Financial disaster was averted but a job vacancy was assured after that and I was at the right place at the right time.

The boss's daughter Wendy was a formidable punter. She would back horses to take out a monkey or a grand and seemed to win on a regular basis. I had no idea where she got her info but wherever it was I was looking forward to sharing the wealth. On the day of the total eclipse in 1999 I worked at Salisbury for Ian Metcalfe, (Jack Bevan) and she took us to the cleaners. To make it worse she was telling us before each bet what kitchen appliance she was going to purchase for her new bungalow. By the end of the day her kitchen must have looked like a Currys showroom or at least it would have had she been able to purchase and get delivery before the last, which of course she couldn't.

My first day's work with the firm was at Bath where they

had a rails pitch. It was a pretty uneventful affair but I got the strength of the firm where they described the £1400 or so they won, as 'just about getting the exes.' For my previous two firms and any others that I had worked for that would have been a very good day's work. There was one thing I did get wrong on my first day. In the past I always used to like getting dressed up for my previous firms, camel coat, Barbour, trilby, flat cap, nice suit etc. I wore my best kit for my first day, before racing Wendy took me to one side and offered the advice, 'We don't wear suits on this firm, we are here to work not be flash' and then casting her eyes around the racecourse, added 'Most of the people in the flashiest suits owe us.' I was quite taken aback because the young sharp-suited guys who always wore 'clickity' shoes and called in big '£1000 to' bets 'down to me' although they rarely even nodded to me, were envied in my eyes. I have to admit having a warm feeling inside to find out that for all the bravado it was all a bluff.

The firm had horses in training over the years with some good stables. I won't go into the names because I'm trying to write this so that nobody gets the needle with me. It's already happened in the past, but I will leave the juice until later. There was an amusing story when they delivered a horse to a very prestigious yard. It's fair to say that none of the family are particularly concerned about sartorial elegance so maybe you could just about forgive the trainer's wife who shouted at the 'stable girl' who was in fact the millionaire farmer's daughter to 'Stay out of the house and know her place.' I'm told that there was temptation to load the horse back in the box, but it was a long way back to the farm in Dorset.

The anticipation of becoming very wealthy on the back of all the information I was going to get was a bit much to bear, but it didn't take long for the first big punt to come through. Wendy always went to the paddock before racing and we didn't start betting until she had returned with her 'circles', marks in the card around the names of the horse she liked the look of in the paddock . This particular day, and it was only in the first week of my new job we were betting at the pre-all-weather Kempton Park. She came back clutching her racecard huffing and puffing with excitement. She had just seen one of the firm's old trainers, not the one who almost banished her from the house. He had a runner in the next, a very tricky looking sprint handicap, 'You can have what you like on it' she puffed with uncontained excitement, before adding 'He said he's a certainty.' This was the sort of news I'd been wanting to hear. Even better that the horse was 8/1 in the ring, that was £1000-£120 for people with money (£2000-£240 for Wendy) I didn't want to look like the poor cousin or indeed miss out so rummaged around in my pocket for the money I had, around £62 counting the shrapnel. That was a £500-£60, a massive bet for me, but I was in the big league now and had been given a tip from a yard that from the stories I had been told from Wendy, never left it behind.

The bookie who took my bet was a bit confused that I paid the bet on, then quizzed me as if the bet was for me. I answered in the positive then gave him a bit of a contemptuous look when he asked if the horse was fancied. It was a daft question after all. They were off and so was I, about to join the ranks of those who effortlessly followed up information courageously and walked away from the tracks with large amounts of readies stuffed into each pocket on a habitual basis. I positioned myself on the joint to watch the race, not for any sense of entertainment of course, after all this was just business, but just to see how far the good thing was going to win, and of course give the obligatory 'Aye Aye' rub-down in the general direction of the rest of the bookies when the horse won.

The animal we backed was conspicuous by its absence from the commentary, I was slightly nervous at this point. £60 was a huge bet. Of course it was only lent but I didn't really want to lose. Perhaps sensing my apprehension Wendy told me not to worry because the horse always came late. By the time they passed us the animal still not mentioned or sighted would have had to have been Pegasus reincarnated to have won, it wasn't and didn't, finishing stone cold last. The feeling was totally gutting. I stood shell-shocked with my pockets feeling decidedly empty and my heart sinking slowly, only to plummet when I saw her grin and exclaim that it was lucky her 'Saviour' won the race. Most people I knew if they had a small bet on the perceived danger to their selection to recoup their stake on their main bet called it a 'saver.' Also most people who I knew didn't have savers or even saviours in races where they had been told that their main bet was a certainty that they could have what they liked on.

I looked at her in disbelief but was too new to the firm to feel able to take issue. Besides, they can't all win as they say. It was a lesson learned, at least for the day. I was hoping that it was just a blip, after all I was always being regaled with tales of tilts at the ring, fortunes lost, horses never in danger. Of course the money was only lent, a short blip on the road to glory.

The firm was an eye-opener compared to what I was used to. The original boss, Ivor, who although having retired was still very much on the scene and keen to look into the book and make sure it was looking as he would have had it, every favourite losing a chunk. That was the sort of book that would have worked back in the day when business was brisk along with some of the other old-school who had the favourite taking out a nice few quid with the second-in taking the book. It was very exciting when you knew that some serious money was at stake, though not so when they won, one after another. And day after day they did. Short-priced winners that Jo made a certainty and not just from guess work but hours and hours of nightly form study. The frustration was palpable, especially when a short one eventually got beaten, despite a string of them having just sauntered effortlessly home costing the firm fortunes a pop.

Some of the bets we took with that firm made the day's racing very exciting though, not to mention the characters who bet with us who didn't with the previous more modest layers. The size of the bets didn't really mean that the info was any stronger. For a short while the bookmaking father of a top trainer used to bet with us. He was a wealthy man but couldn't resist backing his son's horses when he thought they were good things. The old adage about never backing odds-on was blown out of the water with his bets; if he had £50 on at 2/5 it would win. Regardless of the price I always used to follow him in and watch his selection slosh home, small fish are sweeter as Jack Lynn used to say. Needless to say we always used to make sure he was returned the best price so he'd keep betting with us and mark our card. The rule about standing favourites for two grand was also waived, much to the delight of Jo. The real inside info which really was exceptional didn't last very long because he fell ill and sadly passed away within a year of my work starting.

There was a rails bookmaking firm that were feared for backing short-priced certainties on the flat. The father was a very well-respected gentleman whose son was sent out to punt the horses. If he took 6/4 you could be sure that they would be odds-on at the off, while they didn't always win they would always go very close so although we used to always lay him I was always trying to get in front of him to hedge the bets. I did hatch the idea of whatever I had back to ask for the boss's back bet plus my own place. I'm not sure it would have gone down too well with the other bookies but I doubt if I'd ever have not drawn the place money.

There was a larger than life punter who used to like to bet short ones, quite often if there looked to be just two in the race with realistic chances. He'd bet them both to maybe coupled odds of 1/8, the books generally didn't mind laying him. He more often than not won but it was the bumper pay day if they both got beaten. He was a handy man to have about because it was always the job to get the short ones in the book before chasing out the others. He went by a moniker rather than his real name. He had a guy who used to help him stick on, who later became a professional punter in his own right.

There were some real characters with whom I had a lot more contact with the new firm. One guy was one of the last tic-tac men still working. He'd charge £7 for his card and then use 'his' bookies if he was given any business from his phone customers. He'd hop off his box and call bets in along the line. You'd lay him if it suited you and that would be fine. One thing he used to do that really did prove to be ahead of his time was offer to back horses at 1-10 when they had one to jump. Occasionally they would get beaten and he would get pilloried mercilessly but realistically that only happened on very few occasions. Looking back in hindsight with people betting 1-50 and shorter in running in the same position today he probably got himself quite a nice few quid.

The other thing about Ivor Perry and Co was that unlike other firms I had worked for they used to take hedging or shortening up bets on the telephone. We had a special ringtone for those calls, a circus theme, the reason being that's how we looked quite often after we had taken the call. I loved it when I heard that call. Some of the business was simple hedging so we may or may not have moved some of it on. The one I used to love was when the firm on the end of the phone wanted one shortened up. That was great fun, especially when you were just given a sum and told to get the horse as short as possible. You had to be careful not to have a lump on with a firm who just might stand it all though. The trick was having just enough on each time to get other firms hedging and start a domino effect. The other advantage we had is that the ones we backed tended to run very well so the books were pretty cautious about taking the bets on.

It was a bit weird working on course for over a decade. A lot more people started to be friendly now that I was working for a rich hard-hitting firm. I hadn't changed a bit but some people, mostly people who were doing a job no more than mine suddenly thought I was worth talking to. It's funny how people who worked for bookies used to self-adopt the status of their bosses. That was the downfall of a lot of bookmakers' staff. They could get intoxicated by the sight of what they saw as effortless money. A high roller might come in and have a grand on one then a few minutes later he got four back and they would want a piece of that assumed easy money. The bookies would always take personal bets from other bookmakers' staff because they were ultimately responsible for their actions. If they got into trouble their boss would have to pay if they still wanted to keep employing them. It wouldn't often come to that.

The person in question would often get pulled aside by the bookie he owed and have his debt pointed out to him and told he was limited. Quite often a big debt would be rung up in one afternoon. One guy got into trouble when he decided that his well-marked card pointed to a real each-way bet to nothing in the first. He had a bet bigger than he could really afford each-way on a second-favourite and it was unluckily out of the frame. In a rush of blood to the head he continued to punt heavier and heavier with the same bookie for the rest of the day and ended up owing plenty. You might think that the layer was being irresponsible letting him keep having the bets, but imagine what would happen if the first bet they refused to take won and would have got him out. Better to let him carry on. Weirdly enough the bookie would be hoping that the guy got out too. Nobody wants to be chasing debts, especially from people you know and work with.

The guy eventually paid as and when he could but it

wasn't always the case. With punters especially, you had to be very careful who you gave credit to. The trouble was that even though it wasn't intended to do so, allowing credit often crept in. You'd get to know the punter who'd have decent bets. Then one day he'd call a bet in over the heads of other punters and he'd either win or pay no problem. Calling in bets and paying after the race would become the norm which would normally be fine.

There would be the invariable bad day and the punter would go on the missing list. This would be a warning sign but left you with a conundrum because the punter would invariably come up to you the very next meeting with the money outstanding and the process would continue. If you were getting plenty from the punter you wouldn't want to lose the business. Occasionally the punter would go on the missing list for longer. You'd fear the worst, especially if the missing list just meant being in the Silver Ring. If the punter came into a few quid and missed betting in the main ring he'd normally come along and pay, all apologetically, then start over again. You wouldn't want to offend him after he paid, so the cycle would run again.

Not many people knocked us but one guy did and it turned out that he had a history of it. It was particularly galling because, by that time, I was on the stool taking the bets and he was a friend of a friend. He was as big in stature as he was in ego. It was the latter that was the bigger however. He would march to the joint when particularly busy then stand at the back of the gaggle or queue, depending on the nature of the crowd, then boom out, 'Simon, number 9 to win £2000.' This usually resulted in everyone turning around to see who this huge punter was. To the uninitiated it sounded as if he had just had a two grand bet. He'd stand there with his chest puffed out soaking up his moment of glory before turning on his heel, hands in pockets, and heading back to whence he came. I'd then look down to the clerk and say, number 9 £30 with the fractions. (66/1) It seemed very likely to me that he was actually just paying that £30 for those brief moments when a few total strangers took notice of him.

We found out afterwards that his favourite trick was knocking and left a string of bookies out of pocket. Generally he'd draw when he won then leave owing for a while then feign an argument, which could be little more than the bookie having the audacity to chase up his debt and then refuse to pay on the strength of it. He had used that one before with a telephone credit firm. He'd rack up a decent debt then call asking for a price on a horse that had long gone, often with the fractions then explode when he was inevitably refused and tell them that they could swing for their debt.

Even though it wasn't my money I felt responsible and also very annoyed to see him marching around to this day knowing that he owes all over the place.

For every punter of dubious and downright deceitful nature there are plenty of gentlemen that proliferate racecourses. Back during this time there were a good handful of professional punters who were a joy to deal with on a daily basis. I won't give names as in keeping with the rest of this book but two that spring to mind had a penchant for facial hair and are still plying their trade on course today. They had a totally different approach to their punting. As you find with most punters who actually win they do so in a discreet manner. The loud ones tend to be so because when they have a winner, they needed it badly. The first 'beard' is a real gentleman, tall and elegant, as elegant as you can be in practical boots and trousers, a fishing waistcoat and if need be an all-encompassing cagoule. His forte is national hunt racing and he travels the country taking long loping strides around the betting rings.

Before the exchanges came along and changed everything his bets would have affected the market at the smaller meetings, betting in thousands often on multiple selections. It is often said that true professionals do their winning quietly. That is certainly true with this bearded gentleman but not so his losing. If he thought he had seen a poor ride or heaven forbid a race where it looked as if one or two of the horses hadn't really been all out to win, you would see him from a distance bobbing toward the ring. That bobbing would appear more of a bounce as his long loping walk had transformed into a massive bouncing stride covering vast ground. By the time he had reached the bookmakers the first one to mention the race or result would invariably get the benefit of his opinion fairly vehemently put.

He was well liked, knew the bookmakers who would take his sized bets and called in what he was after accordingly. He was not one of those who would ask a small book in the back row for a four-figure bet and then scream the place down when of course he didn't get it. Happily for karma purposes these types generally go skint. This beard rarely got angry when he got knocked back but this was different on one occasion. The day in question was at Kempton Park long before it became an around the calendar all-weather course.

The TV cameras were in the betting ring, our hero was trying to back his selection at 5/2 when suddenly he heard a big booming voice called '£11,000 - £4000' the horse he was after. In a matter of strides he was at the bookie who was enjoying his spot in the limelight still calling '£11,000 - £4,000', so busy playing up to the crowd in front of the TV camera and personality he didn't notice the beard pop up under his arm (the best bet to approach a bookie you think might bluff you) and say he'd have the bet. Much to his indignation the bookie glanced down at him looking slightly uncomfortable and took a flurry of small bets from punters as keen to get on the telly as he was. 'Yes' said the beard, 'I'll have that', once again he was ignored. The third time he asked was louder, luckily the camera crew disappeared, as did the price. Quite miffed now, the beard ask the bookie, who by now uncharacteristically quiet, if he was on.

The bookie shifted a little awkwardly, bent over and whispered that he had only been shouting it for the camera. Incandescent with rage our man spun on the spot and was away. Nobody can remember if the horse won or lost but the memory of the bluff lingers and is still passed on, hence it being included in these pages. Back in those days I often used to give him a lift from Exeter racecourse to the railway station. One day on the drive back to the station he was not quite as chirpy as usual so it was probably a bit foolish to ask if he had a good day. He hadn't, he'd lost over £20k. That was a not 'just not quite as chirpy' loss, that's stoic for you.

The other beard-loving pro-punter keeps such a low profile that he probably won't linger here for long either but has to have a mention. Baseball hatted and with a massive pair of binoculars he has been active in the ring under both codes for as long as I can remember. He is always polite, always pays on and gives nothing away about himself, his business or if he'd won or lost. Maybe that's a boring paragraph to some, to me it's one of the more intriguing.

# Chapter 13

*A Vibrant Place To Be.*

Back in the early 'noughties' the betting ring was a vibrant place with little gaggles of punters that came and went, which is how it tends to go. The Gambling Gods appear to have a bit of a tactic luring people into the world of thinking punting is easy. They arrive on the scene in a blaze of glory. The bookies sometimes think that the new punter has found the much-sought source of quality information and start looking for a pattern. There generally isn't one. They have a sequence of luck then up their stake before they realise the reality of inevitable long losing runs.

One chap who did make a big impact and was a genuinely excellent form student was said to have been of Eastern European origin. His speciality was sorting out big-priced horses with a chance. He'd run around the ring backing outsiders to win grands to the fractions to quite large amounts. A lot of books liked to lay the rags but it soon became apparent that if this guy backed one of them they warranted a second glance at least. Those bets weren't his only tactic. On some occasions he and his little army of shadows would often take on one horse. Before the advent of the exchanges they would back the field against the selection they didn't fancy. They would be betting well odds-on but the guy was obviously very shrewd because the collective cheer that rang out when the horse looked beaten in a race was a regular one.

This tactic led to a busy ring and good business for the bookies. One of the guy's disciples went on to be a very well-respected pundit and punter in his own right. As for the form book guru himself, he briefly went into racehorse ownership before falling off the radar, apparently deciding that winning by form book study alone is impossible as the game is too bent. Luckily I'd like to think I know for a fact that is not true. I can feel his frustration though especially as some blatant, at least to me, offences seem to occur on a daily basis but go totally unpunished.

Because Ivor Perry and Co had a reputation for taking big bets some punters made a point of betting with us to save the hassle of being bluffed. Others of course went to the smaller bookies just for some sort of weird self-gratification. There were a couple of regular punters who, even though they had great winning days, you knew were destined for the poor house and not Ascot in a topper care of their punting. As inexplicably seemed to be the norm both came into the ring as if from nowhere and could do no wrong backing winner after winner. In those cases we always tried to get to know who they were and what the strength of their information was, if indeed they were getting their card marked. One of the guys was a big Welshman who would have £400 every time he had a bet, which was almost every race at regular meetings.

Nobody can win betting like that, so of course we'd accommodate him. The idea would be to keep them betting with you because there was nothing more galling than paying someone a couple of grand only to see them lose it back again just up the line. We'd make sure that he was on over the heads of other punters and call him over if the price had just gone and he walked past us looking for it even it was a bad loser. That might sound clinical but he was getting the very best chance of winning, being offered the best terms and could stop at any time. We had terrible losing days from that one punter many times, though he always paid in cash and kept coming for a long time before going on the missing list. In the long run we did beat him. It was a bit of a sad job really when someone you sort of got to know and liked was obviously losing, but for all we know he could have been fabulously wealthy and just enjoyed a punt for a pastime.

Another guy who bet with us a lot was always going to lose. He used to run around with a copy of The Sun in his back pocket betting short-priced favourites in thousand pound bets. He'd often bet the second favourite each way too which was always going to end in tears. Seeing him squinting at Templegate's tips between races then getting another grand out of his pocket to have on the next race always gave you hope that you'd beat him. The story was that he was a very successful independent house builder whose betting tank used to swell every time he sold a house. Not surprisingly he was rarely seen in the ring after 2008.

Not all of the punters I got to know during that time would lose or go missing but one much-loved character who was the scourge of the ring for decades was tragically killed on the way home from the races. He used to get his card well-marked and march about in the ring calling bets in and lambasting and berating bookmakers for their skinny prices. Sadly (typical of the attitude of some in the ring), when the shocking news of his death reached whatever betting ring we were in next day a genuinely ashen faced and quite upset floorman told his boss the news. The boss looked equally taken back and with trembling voice replied, 'Oh no, that's terrible, did he owe us?'

The size of the bets that the new firm took hadn't really taken me by surprise because everyone knew that they were big layers but it was Cheltenham that really opened my eyes. In the years previously the festival really was something to look forward to and a case of how much your boss was going to win. I was really looking forward to seeing how the new team worked. For starters it was going to be the first time that I had worked the festival in Tatts proper. That is where the real money was changing hands and for once we were going to be fairly small fish in a much bigger and more perilous pond.

The 'pick' the firm had was a very good one that would have put them in a very good position on the front line. Inexplicably to me they opted to bet number one in the back row. The idea was to take the money that was going to come hedging from the rails and from the punters who came from the gate in the bottom of the rail. The problem with the former was that if the money came flooding in from the rails it was likely to be lively. It was the festival after all and nobody really wanted to unload 'hard shouted for' field money. The second problem was that the gate in the bottom of the rail had been closed. In addition to that the way the big screen was positioned meant that people started to put themselves for a good view of the screen and were soon engulfing us, making it very hard to take bets in that important time just before the off.

The position and the meeting was a disaster, the results were diabolical, favourites and well-backed horses with no respite. One short one that we had gone with, looked certain to win when falling two out. The pitch was a terrible one but Ivor dug his heels in for two days, really for no other reason than he had always bet there. Turnover was not a whole lot better than a normal day and strength in depth was missing. The books were totally lopsided with the short ones losing thousands.

Finally we moved on the last day and bet on the front row. It was too little too late but the right decision for sure. Turnover and books were better but such was their style of betting, as the short ones were winning one after the other, the losses mounted to a crippling figure. Stoic until the end the old boss just shook his head after the last, when he looked at the losses figure; well above the national annual yearly salary for the UK he just shook his head, pushed his flat cap and said 'Today would be a good day to get mugged in the car park.'

Another legendary bad losing day was at Ascot just

before Christmas. The meeting had looked in serious doubt due to a very hard frost. It was one of those where the stewards decided to look again and again, virtually everyone expected the meeting to be off. If the grass in the car park was any sort of guide being off was a certainty. All of that illustrated just how wrong you can be however as the meeting finally got the go ahead. We had been having a fairly good run and this was the last meeting before Christmas. Ivor was there and quite active in the decision making. I could tell that Jo feared the worst as his computer screen was being closely monitored with 'advice' being imparted as to laying the short one a bit more.

As the meeting went on the short ones went in one after another with AP McCoy riding winner after winner. Before long the offices got involved, no doubt fearing huge mug bet pay-outs of McCoy accumulators. We always used to lay Hills and Ladbrokes. One of the reps came into us and had a modest bet, probably because we were in a poor pitch, one of our very few that could be described as poor. As the rep went on his way Ivor suddenly sprang to his toes chasing him. He returned beaming from ear to ear having managed to get him to bet another grand at odds-on. 'Shame I caught that rep' was his only response as the favourite won with its head in its chest. Jo's face said it all, something along the lines of 'why don't you just sod off', with maybe an Anglo-Saxon F word in place of the sod.

There was yet another short one in the last. Jo and Graham thought it a certainty and, as they didn't have Ivor's ever watchful eye over them, didn't stand it for anywhere near as much as would have been expected of them. Consistency had always been the byword of the firm but in this case it was deemed prudent and so it proved as the horse duly obliged. As it passed the post Ivor appeared as if by magic. You could hear a pin drop as he said 'Oh that's a bugger, I thought we might get that one beat, I laid a £800-£1300 on for you on the rails'

# Chapter 14

*Jackpot!*

It wasn't all doom and gloom despite the firm having a bad run. I am being totally selfish with that comment because I am talking about a great day that 'I' had. It was at Newbury in January 2002. The jumping card wasn't particularly good and the fields were quite small. It was a very cold day so we decided to go inside the stand and have a cup of tea, something that we rarely did. Jo's dad Graham was with us and had done the form for the meeting and sorted one out for the day. I was always quite excited when he came up with one, more importantly when Jo agreed. His dad was always looking for a bet while Jo was looking for a reason not to. What they really needed was a happy medium in between. That way there would have been a few more bets and totally lethal. As it was bets were few and far between so really were, (and still are), nap material when they both agreed.

While we were sat there the TV volume was up quite loud. The announcer was going through the card and mentioning the horses that had been backed on the day. Jo made a note of them and said that some of them were quite interesting as they were not obvious ones but if you looked hard enough you could make a case for them. I decided I'd have a go at the Placepot. I must have been a bit flush because as well as the pound perm for that I for some reason decided to chuck away another four pound something for a 10p perm on the Jackpot. The bet had been in the racing press because it had controversially rolled over after an odds-on banker was thrown out the previous day at Lingfield which was lucky otherwise I probably wouldn't have given it a thought.

As the day went on one after another won and things started getting exciting. Then the banker, the nap bet won after having our hearts in our mouths all through the race as the horse ran in snatches. I had all the other races permed with at least two selections in each race. We had put three in the last. One of them was a non-runner so had the front two in the market with the unnamed favourite. It was getting very serious now because there was only about £2 left in the pool and the total was a nice few quid. The firm decided not to bet on the last even though I was the only one who was actually involved financially. Wendy sent me off to back the two I had in the race so she could roar them home with me.

That was one of the lovely things about that firm, real sports people. When I backed them for her the betting was 4/1 and 9/2 and so it stayed until just before the off when a well-known heavyweight bookie sent his men around the ring backing the original second favourite. And they were off. I had little worry through the race and was in clover coming to the last when the pair I had in the Jackpot jumped the last hurdle clear. I was going to win the Jackpot. Now I just needed it to be the favourite. They went off so tight we had no idea which one it was. It was big money difference because I would have had an extra line had the favourite won the race.

It may sound very greedy to say but was totally gutted when the SP's showed that the horses had flip-flopped in the betting because of the late bookie bets. The original favourite had won but was now second-in. The bookie had done his money but came straight over to me after the race and shook my hand saying it was nice to shake hands with a winner. Despite winning around seven grand I was smiling back at him with gritted teeth because if it wasn't for him I would have been looking at another five.

Two meetings the new firm didn't bet at were Royal

Ascot and Glorious Goodwood, for no particular reason other than the old boss was busy making hay and straw back in the day when he set himself up as a bookie so didn't bother applying for those pitches. This meant that I could indulge in a spot of freelancing at these meetings.

It was welcome extra work but didn't always go to plan. Jim Clarke was a bookmaker in his own right who sometimes worked for the firm and had his own pitch at the Royal meeting. He asked if I'd fancy a day's work with him. As his pitch was a lowly one he had decided to only go to Ladies Day on the Thursday, put the £500 maximum liability sign up and tap away and try and get a day's wages for us all. Everything was going to plan when just as the last couple of horses were going in the stalls a guy went up to the joint with £500 in cash and had it on Frankie Dettori's mount at 4/1. Jim called me in and asked me to get £400 back.

The price was all around us but the last horse had been loaded into the stalls. The first bet I called was in to a biggish firm. I asked for it all and got nothing; they no doubt already had a tidy book and weren't interested. I asked for the lot with the next book purely out of desperation as they were all in the stalls. This bookie called the bet then changed his mind and said I would have just £100. They were off and running, it was impossible to get up to the business end of the ring and to make matters worse the beast in question was in front and going well. I ran back to the joint and told Jim that I had only managed to get £100 on. To his credit he didn't flap but just said that it would make the race more exciting and that we would just have to get the horse beaten. His demeanour got more edgy as the horse continued to lead and nothing appeared to be coming to get it.

As they passed us with less than a furlong to go only an act of God could have stopped it winning, God was not about to jump to the rescue and the book had lost just under £2000 which was a massive sum. Jim didn't say anything but it was written all over his blood-drained face. He just got off the stool and walked silently away in no particular direction as long as it was away. There were only about ten minutes before the next race when he returned, his pallor had returned to something like normal and he just said we had to start somewhere to get it back. We didn't. He never mentioned it again that day, but has reminded me on intermittent occasions to this day. He did offer me some sort of hint of redemption when he alluded that I was no longer at the very top of his black mark book. He noticed my smile then added that I was still very bloody close to it.

# Chapter 15

*The Ring Embraces The Exchanges –*
*They Know Not What They Do.*

It was around this time that something seemingly quite innocuous hit the betting world, an Internet site called Betfair. It had been born in June 2000 and caused little stir on-course to begin with but over the next few years was to transform, and some might say, cause more damage to the betting ring and bookmaking in general than anything that had gone before it.

The betting exchange on-course really raised its head by the way of punters and in a good way. People started to come out of the woodwork. Some of them were known faces but others had come from seemingly nowhere and were having lumps on mainly short ones. This wasn't a bad thing at all because the bookies generally want to get the short ones into their books first and are usually happy to lay them, that's their game after all. They did attract attention though; to a man they were wired up to a telephone and sort of lurked around then and for no particular reason were in like Flynn asking for lumps. This wasn't all that unusual, but before long there were little teams of guys all trying to get on the same horses at the same time, the horses often shortened and ran very well. The layers were confused.

It didn't take long to find out what was going on. It is a rare gambler who suddenly starts to get a nice few quid who can keep it, and how he has managed it, secret. A few beers after racing with a bookie or member or racecourse regular and the cat was out of the bag as to what they were up to. Arbitrage. These 'Arbers' as they soon became christened had found the

Golden Goose. Well it was, but as soon as they started to blab that goose's countdown to being cooked had already started.

What they were doing was very simple. They kept an eye on the market on-line and on-course and utilised the discrepancies that were apparent in those days, before dongles and Wi-Fi, which left bookies in the dark as to what was going on off-course. To be honest though, most bookmakers back then would have scoffed had you mentioned that prices on-line were different than they were on-course. The on-course bookies made the market so why should they care about some geek on the Internet?

Well the answer to that was very simple. In the past, like it or not, trainers, owners and jockeys who wanted to bet (of course none of them used to lay their horses), often had to use a third party or even if not a third party, a bookie. As soon as that bookie had taken the bet his card was marked and an ensuing avalanche of bets for his own profit would follow. It would have been common place for that bookie to offer his valued client the best odds but it wasn't an ideal situation for those in the know, after all, they paid the bills, did the work, rode the horses but the horrible bookies were getting to know and get the money. Add to that, quite often a good lead may only have a relatively modest bet.

Due to their strike rate that modest bet would be magnified hugely as the word spread and people filled their boots which would look like 'massive gambles' by the off. It didn't take long for connections to realise that betting incognito on-line cut out the middle-man. Once the betting exchange idea caught on, it soon became the best indicator of a horse's chance ever. Gone were the days of false favourites and big margins. The exchanges bet to 100% and once all the various factors were financially contributed by form students and people in the know, by the off for the first time ever, the real chance of a horse winning was reflected in those odds. This is where the Arbers stepped in; rapid moves in the exchange market once the live on-course market was active were suddenly very significant.

The man on the course would be in contact with a mate at home who would be on-line and watching the market. In those early days it was quite likely that a horse could go from 2/1 to 6/4 on-line while the guy on-course could still bet 9/4 with a bookie. Depending on how the firm chose to do it they could bet an £1800-£800 and lay a £1200 - £800 online (minus commission). As the market move was no doubt inspired by lively money the strike rate would be high.

The bookies were all of a sudden very vulnerable; laying horses over the odds is never a good idea, especially if the money is inspired. Even worse, 'somebody', they spat, 'was earning off of them.' It wasn't long before the Arbers found themselves confronted with bookies on the phone to a member of staff at home themselves. Not only were they able to see the market moves they could also see the value of an 'arb' so the lively ones were joining in tucking up their brethren. The other kickback was that those bookies in poor pitches who were normally scratching around and frightened to death of taking a decent bet, largely because there was nowhere for them to hedge should they lay one, suddenly found themselves in a position to earn out of every bet.

It wasn't long before people started to complain that exchanges had no place in the betting ring but the genie was out of the lamp. For a while though using the exchanges in the betting ring was banned, which was of course impossible to police. The funniest thing was watching those who had already become dependent on using them going to all sorts of lengths to try and hide the fact that they still were, using disguises that were akin to a funny nose and glasses. There were bookies with men sat in the car out in the car park on the phone to a floorman; there were those who would be seen taking a lumpy bet and then scamper off to the 'toilet', or whisper hurriedly to one of their staff who ran off to the 'toilet.' The more likely scenario was for the bookie to just get on the phone to their man at home on the computer, should anyone challenge him as to who he was calling he would indignantly say he was checking up on how his poor old mum was, which of course was an excuse hard to prove incorrect.

Defeat was soon admitted and exchanges were once again permitted. Not all firms embraced them, ours included. We just carried on in the old way and were finding it harder and harder. The arbing firms used to bet with us because as we didn't use the exchanges we were not conscious of the value they were getting. Besides, what did we care what they were doing with the bet once we had laid them or what price it was on some Internet site. Things started to get worse as times went on. The arbers did fill the gap that was being noticeably left by the professional and habitual punters who had latched on to the exchanges. The trouble was, we were not getting the favourites that turned out to be weak and below par, into the book but were laying the lively ones over the odds on a regular basis. That is a very direct route to the poor house, but the firm had deep pockets and an almost stubborn will not to leave the old ways behind and embrace the way things were going.

Things couldn't go on like it. For the first time ever we started missing meetings, but the 'eureka' moment came at one of the local tracks, Newton Abbot. One of the off-course firms came down the line backing a horse. We laid them at 13/8 to a lump bigger than our confidence-dented funds really wanted to stand and shortened the price to 6/4. Shortly afterwards we heard one of the hitherto smallest layers not just in the ring but the entire country shout 7/4. Wendy jumped off the stool and called in a ridiculous bet for that bookie, £700-£400, she thought he may get a £175-£100 or even a £70-£40 for 'taking the piss', but to his astonishment she laid it all then as he walked away heard the cry 'Do you want it again?' That was the moment it became obvious that things had moved on and that we either had to get on the exchanges or go out of business.

It wasn't in our case a choice that was made lightly. The exchanges had ruined our business as we knew it, but it was a simple case of comply or die. It was quite obvious that things as we knew it would never be the same and that bookmakers had willingly wandered to the edge of the precipice. Catch 22, you knew that in the long-term stepping into it would be a very bad idea, but lurking over your shoulder, albeit only on the horizon at this point was financial ruin. One by one bookies blinked and allowed themselves to be drawn into the abyss.

Other problems the exchanges caused on course were catastrophic even though people didn't seem to realise at the time. The first thing to happen was that bookmakers stopped betting with each other. There were relatively few really big layers at run of the mill meetings. Even those who did customarily take huge bets would baulk in low class races. They would probably take any bet offered but then send their men out hedging so money would filter back through the ring. Even more modest bets would find their way around the ring. If a front row layer took a £1800-£800 and he could see 5/2 in the back row he may well have had a couple of hundred quid back on it to better his overall book. The reason for this was that they could get a fractionally better price for their hedging on the exchanges. This thinking was very short term and set about strangling the ring from within.

Other manifestations of this meant that the circus ring-tone on our phone was heard less and less. Once the liquidity on the exchanges became stronger than the ring it became very difficult to affect a price on-course if there was opposition against it off. One occasion the usually weak market at a Midland jump track simply absorbed four-figures of money sent from off course to try and shorten up a run-up bet with no effect at all. They weren't happy, the firm who had to put it on burned their fingers and it soon all dried up. Genuine hedging money was easily now sorted out on the machine, as it was soon quaintly universally known, so dried up too.

The off-course reps were finding it equally as hard. They were soon totally flummoxed trying to shorten up a 'shop horse.' If there was plenty of money in the exchanges for a horse they would find that the sort of bets that would get the vast majority of the layers running for cover and starting a domino effect were just being swallowed up. The off-course guys were tearing their hair out to find that the bookie they had a £1000 bet with at 13/8 on the way into the ring was screaming 7/4 as he left it. In fact the exasperation was summed up when rather than some bookies doing their best to bluff or cut the firms they could be seen literally chasing reps around the ring, something akin to the closing credits of a Benny Hill show.

The feeding frenzy to earn from the off-course firms was basically a mutual suicide pact with layers blinded by greed as to what irreparable damage they were doing to their own business and environment. If it was possible for fish to drink their own pond dry it would be a perfect metaphor. If this all seems like good news for the off-course punters, it wasn't. Just as the market on-course was effected by strength in the market it was equally so when there was a collapse on-line. Just as in days gone by when the off-course reps used to smash into the ring, a horse being supported on the exchanges would ensure a collapse in the price in the ring, sometimes without a significant amount of money for the beast. The tail was beginning to wag the dog.

The betting ring, a healthy mutual trading centre made up of independents in competition with each other but with mutually assured survival in all their interest, was fast becoming a cluster of black holes funnelling any money it took off-course, slowly diminishing numbers due to wastage on the wings. In addition to this the money coming into the ring was getting less and less as serious punters cut down their expenses by giving up the hustle and bustle of the racecourse for the comfort of their own home, the satellite racing channels and the pale glow of a computer screen. Pretty much overnight the way our firm operated changed from an out and out layer taking on the punters to falling into line with everyone else and using the exchanges as our tool. Jo's Dad was employed to sit at home on the computer and on the telephone to us hedging when necessary and trying to stop us getting nabbed by the arbers. It was decided that should we get caught napping we'd still lay them, maybe not all of their bet but certainly a good chunk of it.

These were much better times. The books that we were making were proper bookmakers books and not just lopsided gambling. We were winning on a regular but modest basis and the stress was off. The big plus side was that in the decent pitches we could field decent money and bet to good figures, in other words proper bookmaking. We had some fun times with our new member of staff sat at home. It became obvious that he was not concentrating entirely on what he was supposed to be doing. We could hear the racing at other courses on the television in the background so were guessing that he would have two pages up, one for him and another for us.

Back in those days the computers were nowhere near as able to deal with multiple tasks as they are today. We'd ask a price for a horse at our meeting then there would be silence then a muffled murmur about there being money for it or that the computer had frozen. It was a bit cruel really but we used to terrify him on purpose when we could tell he was trying to bet one of his own at the other meeting. All joking aside it was a serious business especially if we got nabbed by an arber.

# Chapter 16

*Farmer Bert – You Bazzard You.*

Travelling around was a costly business so I got lifts when I could. I would meet the firm at the Little Chef just past Wincanton on the A303. It was after racing and being reunited with my car that I had a run-in with a wannabe traffic policeman. I had only just set off back towards Devon when I was suddenly in queuing traffic; one thing about the A303 is that unlike the motorway system there are always ways around hold-ups by various duck off roads. I noticed a few going off a tiny road just in front of me so decided to follow. I had no idea where it went but assumed those that had taken it did, plenty of others followed suit.

Things were going OK for a bit. We travelled up for a while then took a right descending to hopefully join the road on the other side of what was causing the hold up. Unfortunately motorists from the other direction were trying to do the same via the same tiny lane, we soon met head on. A guy who I guessed must have been a farmer, well not just a farmer but the farmer from around those parts, was marching up the lane illuminated by headlights telling the cars coming in my direction to stop. He said that there were 'hundreds' of cars coming this way that couldn't go backwards but it was OK if the cars in my direction reversed back and carried on forward for another mile or so where they could duck back down and hit the road.

Those at the back simply reversed, once they had cleared the road we were told to turn around in a gateway. It was pitch black apart from the car headlights. The first few turned around with no problem, and then it was my turn. The 'farmer' pushed his flat cap back on his head and shouted at me to reverse into the darkness, 'Back, back, back' he ordered, then as I complied to the fourth 'back' my car suddenly dipped at the rear. I tried to pull forward but it was evident that I was stuck. The farmer looked exasperated, I jumped out of the car to see that I was sunk right up to the wheel arch in mud, no chance whatsoever of driving out. The 'farmer' didn't seem too bothered. I was far enough off the road that the cars coming in his direction could get past and get on their way.

He obviously had a trusty tractor parked in top field that he could use to extricate me from the position he had got me in. The cars coming my way had all gone and those from farmer's side streamed past, some of them cast me a glancing frown possibly assuming I had been the cause of the hold up. I was stood next to farmer also assuming in my case that he was just waiting for the traffic to clear before he got me out. I was a little taken back when a battered old car with three other 'farmer' types in it pulled up and shouted to the 'farmer.' I forget his name but he looked like a Bert so that's what I will call him. 'Come on Bert' they cried, so Bert who it suddenly dawned on me wasn't the farmer, and maybe not even a farmer at all but just dressed like one, jumped in the car without giving me a second glance and they drove off. Bastards!

So there I was, it was pitch black and raining. I was up to the buffers in mud and had no idea where I was. I did have a mobile phone luckily, but no signal. There was no option but to walk until I could get one. I also had no idea if the AA did rescues so I tried to ring the boss. Still no signal. They had tractors but I didn't know where I was. Eventually, as I made my way up the hill I got a bar. I tried the boss again, answer phone. I left a message, telling of my predicament and a pause followed by 'bastards.'

The AA it was then, and for your information, they do

rescue stuck drivers but it is handy if they know where you are. I couldn't tell them, so walked until the crossroads where I remembered a sign. It was so dark I had to use the light from my phone screen to read the words letter by letter. The person on the end of the phone decided to patch me straight in to the nearest AA driver. I wasn't much help. These days I know that road very well and could have told him pretty much exactly where I was.

The AA are indeed the motorist's mate. They eventually found me and managed to pull me out. Pretty much as I got back on the road, cold and wet, I got a call from a very entertained boss. They had fallen about laughing at my message, especially the long pause followed by 'bastards.' I'm glad they thought it was funny, thanks for that 'Bert.'

For a brief period I actually did start to get some proper inside information, just a tantalising glimpse into that mysterious inner circle that is said to exist in racing. There certainly seem to be people who are always on the live ones and also seem to know exactly what is going on. This is the money that used to be thrown like a hot potato from bookie to bookie before the advent of the betting exchanges. I attended a 30th birthday party in London where I met a few guys who worked in Internet betting. They impressed me with their stories of their 'shrewdies' and following their bets in, making great profits.

What one particular guy told me was that they had a handful of red-hot punters who they followed. They won from the firm but rather than close their accounts as traditionally happens, with the big firms they just limited them. Not too much but down to £100 or so. That way it was still worth their while to bet with the firm and all the staff. The firm of course had their cards marked with information that would have been priceless in the right hands. The guy was rather drunk but offered to give me his number so I could call him and he'd let me know what the 'shrewdies' were on at the meeting we were going to.

The information was different class. They didn't all win but they were pretty much all triers. I decided to have £20 a time on these bets and would decide what to do with the pile of money I was going to amass holidaying on a tropical island somewhere. I won a nice few quid to begin with but was soon to learn a lesson. No matter how good the info is you are going to get a bad losing run. In this case an unbelievable run of twenty consecutive seconds, not losers, seconds, one place better they would have all won and I'd have won a fortune, but they all came second so I lost £400, which was plenty to me back then. I decided to halve my stakes to a tenner, the very next bet won at 20/1. You couldn't make it up and I haven't, but it was a lesson. The info didn't last long, the firm went to the wall and the guy moved on. It was like having a peek behind the green door at the rocking party just for a few seconds before having it slammed in your face again.

# Chapter 17

*The Form Genius That Proved Gambling Can Pay – Mounty.*

Two meetings that we used to attend regularly were Hereford and Worcester. It was there that I met a chap that was going to become a great friend and the proof that it was possible to make it pay by pure hard work studying form. Andrew Mount was working with the Martyn of Leicester firm at the time. Martyn is a larger than life character with a natty if limited line of cheesy patter trying to call in the punters. 'Money without work' being a perennial favourite. Andrew was the total opposite, very unassuming and quiet. However, he came alive when talking about horses and form and would produce reams of paper full of facts and figures to back up a case he was making for a horse. He also ran a tipping service called 'Trend Horses' and wrote two books a year of the same title.

Bearing in mind my previous experience with tipsters had been make-believe characters like Ryan Hartley and Wendy's exaggerations, I wasn't too excited when he said he'd add me to his friends and family list for free access to his bets, but was impressed with the book and set to work reading it. By this time I had pretty much given up betting. I had done my cobblers following Wendy, (but that was of course my choice for not having a pop). Jo's bets were profitable to follow but very few and far between. I found I was skint a lot less when not betting. For a time I didn't even read the emails not wanting to be tempted in to betting and losing again but did look out for the horses and their trends.

I'm not sure how long that was, but it wasn't  that long

before lazy Simon realised Andrew did all the work for you with his tipping service, in addition to his daily form study and skill interpreting it. I began by just having £2.50 per suggested bet point on his tipping service mainly on the exchanges. I'd have the bets and forget about them but was amazed to see how my tank was growing. He was having a very purple patch at the time and the tank grew and betting became fun again. Of course it didn't last in that way for ever and a trait of Andrew's, as well as anyone else who backs horses, was a back down to Earth with a bump on a regular basis, losing run. My stakes gradually grew, every bet was recorded and profit was being shown.

Part of Andrew's problem was that due to the nature of traceable betting on-line he was either closed down or vastly limited so had problems getting on. I had plenty of hardly-used accounts so started to place bets on his behalf as well as my own. I opened accounts I didn't already have so we could get on at best prices. It didn't take long for the profits to start rolling in and the accounts to be trimmed as a result. Those limits continue today, long after that brief period of success.

We were particularly unlucky with one independent, Andrew wanted to get a monkey on a horse, I had opened an account for him as a recommendation, they laid him £300 at 10/1, I had the other £200 on at the price. The horse was beaten by a short-head at 9/4. We had lost £500 but from that day on any bet we tried to get was at least worst price on the Oddschecker website. It was never official but I sometimes used to call and ask a price just for a bit of entertainment and to see if my account was still marked, it was.

Andrew was also very helpful with my writing. At the time I was covering the local meetings for the Mid-Devon Gazette series again. I wasn't getting paid but really enjoyed writing those columns. I used to try and find a story about the personalities in the ring and at the races to relate rather than a series of results. You could get them anywhere. Before long the readers were familiar with some of the people in the ring, Balertwine Barry, Armaloft Alex and Meldrew the miserable bookie. The idea seemed to be working because I used to get a wide range of people stopping me saying how much they enjoyed reading my column even though they weren't interested in racing, even adding that it made them want to go along.

It was thanks to Andrew that I got to write similar stories in a national publication. He met the editor at the launch at a racecourse and had a word with him. I sent him a trial 2000 words and in issue 2 was part of the landscape of Racing Ahead. Bit between my teeth I was also accepted writing reviews from the betting ring for The Racing Post Weekender starting with a generic piece on the betting ring then regular reviews from the big meetings we attended, Royal Ascot, Goodwood and Cheltenham. I was extremely proud to be published in the Weekender. I remembered very well buying the very first issue in 1983 which at the time had a columnist named Jeffrey Bernard writing for them. I loved his booze sodden take on the game; I hoped to emulate his column without the self-destructive alcoholism part.

I was really ambitious and confident about myself feeling no fear of rejection. I was rejected on a regular basis by the Racing Post but I continued to pester them like a terrier. I was also still working on a freelance basis for the bookies so was immersed in racing.

# Chapter 18

*Scoop 6 Glory.*

I got a call from Andrew one Saturday morning asking if I could get anyone interested in chipping in for a tilt at the Scoop 6. I phoned around and got a few people to invest £20 a piece including myself. We were working at Stratford that day but after the first couple of winners most of our attention was on the Scoop 6. Race by race we were still in and by the last had won it, though along with several others.

The bonus was going to be at Newbury the following week. Only 5 people picked Short Skirt in the feature race and Andrew was one of them. We were at Chepstow that day so piled into the betting shop to watch the race. The place erupted as Ryan Moore took up the running well inside the final furlong. The win was only a couple of grand but the start of an excellent run of Scoop 6 and Jackpot wins Andrew had for us.

# Chapter 19

*Much-Loved Characters That Have Come And Gone.*

The firm was doing well again due to the total change of tactics so it was a good time. The old boss Ivor didn't come racing every day but enjoyed joining us for the bigger meetings when we stayed away. He was of the old school, he believed in cash and keeping hold of it. There were quite a few stories abounding about his old style of laying and how fearless he was. He still liked to carry a bundle. One of the tales about him was when he was boarding a plane to the Channel Islands. He had to empty his pockets for security and took out a house brick sized wedge and nonchalantly placed about £2k in used notes beside his car keys. The security lady's eyes opened widely and asked why he had such a large amount of money on him, to which he replied, 'It may be a large amount of money to you my dear.'

A similar tale was told to me by trainer David Elsworth, once again involving Ivor's penchant for cash rather than embracing the card system of the 21$^{st}$ century. He was due to be going racing with the trainer to watch his horse after flying in that morning. David Elsworth recorded that he got a call about an hour before he was expecting him. Ivor was at the airport but hadn't been able to pick up his hire car as planned. The trainer asked why not, 'I don't know' was the reply, 'They say that they want a credit card, I haven't got a credit card.' He added that he was puzzled, and told the guy on the desk that even though he didn't have a credit card he did have a grand but they wouldn't take it. 'I'd best come pick you up' was the exasperated reply, knowing that of course that meant he'd have to take him back too. While on the subject of grands, Ivor didn't really seem to like spending them too much.

This was a trait that never went unnoticed; Ian Metcalfe often picked up on it when we stayed away together. Ivor would be a little slow in putting his hand in his pocket and would also be slightly difficult when it came to eating out. He would always ask if they could do him a fried egg to put on his steak, regardless of the quality and serving. He was also pretty much certain to ask the bemused waitress about the quality of the cheese board option. The waitress would more often than not go through a list of the cheeses that lay on it only for him then to ask 'But are they tasty?'

One occasion had Ian, and fair to say the rest of those present, speechless. Our party had been a relatively small one so it was obvious that after standing back but accepting drinks for the rest of the rounds it was finally Ivor's turn to pay. 'On you then' goaded Ian with a smile, that smile grew broader as one of the familiar house brick sized wad of notes was rummaged out of a tweed trouser pocket, then after a longing look he returned it from whence it came and said 'I would do but I don't want to break into a grand!' Of course, with the advent of internet betting the days of firms and individuals carrying large amounts of cash are long gone.

This was a happy time where I got to know some of the South West's favourite betting ring characters. I wrote about them regularly in my column in the Mid-Devon Gazette and they seemed to enjoy it. One bookie, Johnny Deane was a spitting image of Richard Wilson better known as Victor Meldrew from the popular TV series 'One Foot In The Grave.' Not only was he like him in looks but had the demeanour to match. No matter how good the winning day he'd be deadpan. He was also the master of the bluff when you called in a back bet request. His tactic was to glaze over and gaze over your head, then when you eventually questioned if you were on he'd point to some hapless chap just lighting a fag and say that he'd done it there. This would leave the fag lighting fella wondering what bet he'd just had, but he too would be ignored should he have the temerity to ask. I wrote a piece about him one day when the layers had a terrible day with all six favourites obliging. He'd backed them all in an accumulator and got himself a nice few quid. He proved he could smile that day, a big beaming one.

Things didn't always go his way however. At Chepstow one Friday evening a punter was stood swaying from side to side obviously inebriated, as were coachloads as was usual on a Friday night. 'Meldrew' had just changed a price on the board, shorter of course. With this the swaying guy fumbled about and found a fiver in his pocket and lurched towards the pitch asking to invest it at the price he had just removed.

Of course, Meldrew wasn't having that, the guy was annoyed at being refused so thought up a unique way of retribution. He once again reached into his jeans, but this time his penis appeared and he started to piss in very imaginative patterns all over the joint. Meldrew's wife was ashen-faced, the picnic she had prepared was stored behind the pitch and little yellow foaming rivulets started to meander their way toward it. As she busied herself trying to rescue the sandwiches Meldrew just stood there, well not exactly stood, but danced about avoiding the splashes. 'Blimey, that must have been his first one of the day' remarked a disgusted but none the less tickled-pink neighbouring bookie. Luckily for justice the long arm of the law had time to spot what was going on and arrest the unruly urinator before his recycled beer made the second row.

Ian and Diane Metcalfe were a lovely couple who I got to know very well. They were third-generation bookies from Torquay. They had taken over the pitches when Ian's father died. He had been working in his shadow for years so now relished the opportunity to bet in his own right. They had given me odd bits of work over the years when I was not required by my other firms. That wasn't often because we generally bet at the same tracks though generally had much better pitches.

I was sometimes used when there were no clashes which meant my usual firms would give the meeting a swerve. The firm was founded in 1897. Ian had a cherished photograph of the firm betting at Torquay races off the back of a horse and carriage around those time. The logo and even font unmistakable, he was very proud of that. Their longevity in the ring was the official reason why they had such good pitches and seniority. Jack Lynn said that it was true but added that before the BPA when bookies organised themselves with waiting lists and rules the razor gangs used to run the pitches and ask for a bob in the pound. The founder of the firm used to pay double and in doing so gained much more than he was paying and everyone was happy. Of course all those people are long-since dead now so I'm going to choose to believe it.

Ian sprang into the spotlight after the infamous incident in 1997 when a 'bookmaker' going by the name of 'John Batten' did a runner from Epsom Downs. For those who don't know the story, 'John Batten' stood in the unregulated part of the racecourse and took bets all day on the Derby offering very competitive odds on the odds-on favourite Entrepreneur. At some point during the race the team up and left with all the money leaving a couple of guys they had picked up as workmen on the day guarding the abandoned kit.

The irony was that had they stayed or come back they may have had a great winning race because the aptly named Benny The Dip won the race at 11/1 with the favourite only 4th. It would have been a lot worse for the betting public had the favourite won but of course all those who had backed the winner didn't get paid. You had to have a sneaking admiration for the audacious team when it was noticed that the code word on their tickets bore the legend 'Lucan.' The reason Ian was brought into the spotlight was because in the course of the police investigation one photograph emerged of 'John Batten' and there was a definite similarity.

The image wasn't clear at all but an SP man made a tongue in cheek suggestion to the Racing Post that the vanishing bookie looked very much like Ian Metcalfe. Of course it was little more than a wind-up as it was very unlikely that Ian would go incognito in any betting ring betting in front row pitches all over the west of England. The Racing Post still published an article linking Ian to 'John' with photos of the pair side to side in the paper. They were accompanied with a vehement denial from the boss of the Bevan organisation who luckily had several thousand alibis as they had been betting at the Umberleigh point to point meeting which was the sun-kissed finale of the season. Needless to say no charges were forthcoming and everyone had a great laugh. As far as I know 'John Batten' was never found, disappearing without trace into racing's murky rogue-laden folklore.

As we had good pitches in our area after Ivor bought up we bet next to them at places like Taunton, Exeter and Newton Abbot so a friendship with Ian and Diane was forged. They would often stay away with us at meetings and go out for meals etc. They featured in many of my articles for various reasons.

Ian had a very unique way of goading his customers in to have a bet, almost taking the micky out of them as to how rich he was and that he'd be getting their wages again before the week was out. Some of his calls to his punters involved how they had all helped pay for his house on the hill and that you wouldn't beat his prices, not even at Tesco. That was originally used at Newton Abbot where the superstore is just across the road but could soon be heard all over the west of England.

There seemed to be a real love hate relationship with a lot of the punters who bet with Ian. He'd smile at them through gritted teeth as they tried to blag a price then as they span around, sometimes accommodated, sometimes not, he'd mutter 'Fuckin' man' to his clerk. His clerk was quite often Diane who was a lovely lady, always kind, smiling and immaculately turned out. She even got up on the stool to bet in his place when he was unable to work due to a stubborn and on-going problem with his foot. The punters didn't scare her, not even at the London tracks.

It was a terribly sad day when they told us one day at Taunton races that Diane had been diagnosed with terminal pancreatic cancer. It was hard to believe, she still looked young, healthy and radiant. She kept on working for as long as possible and even hosted social events at their house on the hill carrying on bravely until finally succumbing around twelve months later. Ian had been in ill health on a lesser scale for some time too, but was determined to work his pitches despite his grief. I had the pleasure of working the last two Royal Ascots of his life with the firm. His pick was number 3 but we bet number 1 on most occasions where he fielded bets proud as punch to be in that position. Sadly Ian died less than a year after Diane passed away.

One thing marred the last year. A writer from the Racing Post asked him how his day had been. It had been bad he was told, the way the reporter wrote his piece, not intentionally I'm sure, but joking about it having been such a bad day the bookie looked ill (he was) and making a slightly questioning remark about the accuracy of the proudly displayed 'Est 1897' sign on his electronic board upset him quite badly. He never bet at another Royal Ascot but I'm sure those last 5 days were very proud ones.

Another bookmaker no longer with us who I had fond affection for was Brian Edwards. Brian was a life-long bachelor from a bookmaking family. He was also a teacher and keen boxing enthusiast, not taking part, though he was big enough so may have once, but supporter of the Plymouth boy's boxing club. I came into contact with him very early in my career in the ring. He was quite a formidable character who took no nonsense from anyone. And when I say anyone I mean anyone. He was a stickler for doing the right thing and one of those rare people, at least in the betting ring, who would agree with a decision even if it would be detrimental to him.

Brian used to be in charge of the line layout at point to points when I first started. He would bark out instructions to the bookmakers who all fell into line like schoolboys. Even the hierarchy, who were the unwritten rulers on-course, held no fears for Brian which would be exhibited with the occasional 'When I say everybody I mean everybody so that includes you Dave Pipe.' Dave Pipe the hugely revered father of champion trainer Martin would jump with the rest of them. I often thought that I would have hated to have been a pupil in one of Brian's classes.

That was before I got to know Brian. Despite his no-nonsense approach that applied to everyone he was totally fair and had a heart of gold. He also had a good sense of humour chuckling away to himself as he related stories of his past in and out of the betting ring. He was always willing to help out whenever he could. Many a bookie who ran short of readies would have been helped in a flash. Brian did have a few characteristics that would be hard to relate without it seeming like I am taking the mick. I am certainly not but it wouldn't be a rounded memory of Brian not to mention what a wag once described as his collection of 'edible ties.' I always wondered how he managed to have a three course meal on his tie. I found out when he was good enough to give me lifts.

Brian used to drive a people carrier, fast, eating and drinking as he went. If he got into conversation about something he felt strongly about, and that could be a lot of subjects being a passionate and intelligent man, things could get a bit precarious, especially if he had already asked for his coffee. He had a large plastic cup much like one that might be given to a toddler, you know the type, with a lid and a mouth-sized bit for sucking the coffee through. It has to be said that this item did look a bit of a health hazard, slightly grubby and brown where it once was blue. Driving with one hand on the wheel and the other on the coffee was risky enough but if he was hungry too he'd also be tucking into a pasty held with the steering wheel hand.

This was when you had to hope that he didn't get too excited with the conversation. I would be sat in the back trying desperately not to raise his hackles. If I did he would take a noticeable shift in his seat to turn around far to enough to look properly at me and bark his opinion in a spray of coffee and pasty flakes while the people carrier veered in a very worrying manner at speeds approaching 100 mph. There was never an incident however, even when he heard of a short-cut out of Worcester races that he fearlessly took on despite meaning heading down a grass bank that was surely there to stop any vehicle trying just that.

Brian was a member of our Scoop 6 syndicate. He had £20 a go which was the minimum and complained every week that we didn't win. His loyal right-hand man John was also in for the same amount. It was my job to collect the money from everyone. It was a fairly easy job apart from Brian who always berated the selections and Andrew's skill at selecting them. You knew that he was trying to wind you up and that as soon as you turned your back he would be chuckling to himself. After the third time we won the bet the bonus race was The Hennessey Gold Cup at Newbury. We had gone in with the other winners so we had 6 selections. Andrew had picked Air Force One which was the only horse still in with a chance at the business end of the race, not only in with a chance but looked very likely to win as they approached the second last. Hopes were high of a million pound cheque to share. Just as we started to count the money that hope was shattered as David Pipe's Madison Du Berlais, a 40/1 shot wrecked the dream by beating us. We were all stood around feeling deflated then I could see him coming from the nether regions of Tatts, Brian, marching towards us. I just knew what he was going to say, and he did, 'Why didn't you have that one in?'

Brian struggled with prostate cancer for quite some time before succumbing to it. He did come racing from time to time. The last time I saw him he was at Salisbury and looking a little frail but the spirit was still there. I went over and shook his hand and told him that it was nice to see him and asked how he was. Typical of Brian, he seemed happy to see me then said quite brusquely 'I'm OK, it will take more than cancer to kill me' before turning around, conversation over. Sadly this time Brian was wrong, but it had to work really hard to get him, stubborn until the end.

One layer who was a constant source of entertainment was a London-based bookie also no longer with us. He was known as a bit of a rough diamond, a loveable rogue but always fun to be around. He had no qualms about saying what he thought to anyone. Nobody had any 'status' as far as he was concerned. I'll call him MM. If someone turned up in a trilby and he thought it looked daft he'd shout across the ring something along the lines of 'What the fuck do you think you look like?' and after the one time I saw that, I rarely spotted that egotistical bookie wearing it again, though I thought it looked quite smart.

I mentioned before about the tic-tac who liked to bet at long odds-on when a horse looked home and hosed in running. One time when he came unstuck it has to be said he looked hot and flustered stood on his box. I have no idea what he expected to earn that day but he had dropped a nice few quid, a grand at 1/20 if I remember rightly. Of course with MM at the races he wasn't going to be able to live it down. Throughout the day when it was just quiet enough he'd get a loud shout of 'Are you still here?' or 'How many fivers do you have to nick to get that grand back?'

Another of his favourite tricks was to amuse himself with winding up reps. If he saw one of the firms running around taking all the 8/13 about a horse he'd suddenly call out 'Take a £3000-£2000.' The reps would bust a gut running down to him and ask for it, he'd feign amazement and ask what they were after. When they replied the 4/6 he'd just laugh and remove the price. Of course this didn't go down well and they didn't always fall for it, but it kept him entertained.

Another occasion that springs to mind was when a new firm had paid a lot of money for one of the top pitches at Newbury. The day was an absolute disaster for the ring. A virtual full house of well-backed favourites had won through the card. To make things worse it seemed like the new firm were doing their best to take as much money as possible and make a real impact. After the financially crippling last, as each firm packed away their kit in morose silence, that post-battle tranquillity was shattered when our hero looked up and hollered 'Oi,' leaving a pause long enough for the crestfallen team to whom he was referring to look up, before adding 'Welcome to Newbury!' A spontaneous laughter burst out around the ring, with the exception of the guys it was directed at, which made our man grin from ear to ear and forget about the money he had lost.

MM didn't get it all his own way though. One day at Chepstow he bet next to us on a particularly boisterous Friday night. He had either come with little money originally or things had gone horribly wrong but for whatever reason they decided to pack up early. As the team gathered the gear up looking rather miserable they were surrounded by a, let's say rather refreshed, group of young Welshmen. They noticed he was leaving and his general grumpy demeanour so decided to play him at his own game, even though they were probably oblivious to what his game usually was. In doing so they also helped perpetuate a myth, the one that everyone sings in Wales. They formed a semi-circle around him as he struggled to pack his kit into the suitcases provided and started to sing a rousing chorus of 'We've got all your money.' He was quite forthcoming with abuse directing salvos of four-letter words at them, so they got louder, 'We've got all your money', which made him angrier and redder than he already was.

The chorus now escalated into a crescendo as others, who may or may not have had all his money, burst into song too. He then aimed his abuse of them toward us, nodding in the general direction of this impromptu male voice choir and cast aspersions about the gene pool contained within and parental wedlock status. We did our best to ignore them fearing the wrath of the rabble should it look as if we agreed. The choristers themselves appeared to be so delirious in song that they either didn't notice or didn't care what he was calling them.

The more our man hurried the less his kit was cooperating with being put away and the more they sang. Eventually he had gathered enough into cases and bags to make his escape up through the ring followed closing by the singing, clapping and slightly wobbly throng.

# Chapter 20

*Is The Party Nearly Over?*

Once the way the firm worked had changed from laying to bookmaking, with the exchanges as hedging, we were winning, though modestly, on a regular basis. We weren't missing many meetings to begin with but that soon started to change. The problem was that before now each firm had their own way of betting. Some would use their knowledge, either of the form book or well-marked cards, other just lay the favourites or make careful books. That way there was room for everyone. Add to that money from the firms and hedging cash going all around the ring it made for a vibrant market. All of a sudden it was strangling itself from within.

The off-course firms soon got fed up with on-course bookies who would previously only lay modest bets sucking up all they were offered then funnelling it all off-course to the 'machine.' So that money all but dried up. The other smaller firms found it impossible to shorten one up if they wanted to so our circus phone stopped ringing. The exchanges, so briefly a life-line to those back row books who had nowhere to go should they lay a thick one, became their nemesis simply because once the front row books had latched on the money never got past them.

If it wasn't already going downhill fast in Tatts the decision to allow rails bookmakers to display boards was a hammer blow for previously good working pitches. At bread and butter mid-week meetings you could always rely on a nucleus of members to come even though the serious punters had started to drift away to the lure of the exchanges. Overnight those mysterious rails layers who you previously had to ask for their prices and were seen as the bookies for the big punters were user-friendly and accessible to all. Their business changed overnight too. They were not just stood there hoping to lay their clients, either mugs or good leads ideally, but were now betting like Tatts bookies, trying to field money and make books.

With a long line of customer-friendly bookmakers showing competitive prices in the member's enclosure there was very little reason for those members to venture out of their comfort zone in to any other area. Those second or third row picks, that had always been good because of their proximity to entrances to and from members, were suddenly useless. Those bookies who had better picks chose to return to the front rows ousting the previous incumbents who found themselves shifted back into the financial cold of the largely now unworkable second line.

With things getting tougher more and more emphasis was being put onto what was happening on the 'machine.' Some layers were getting totally obsessed by it. They had changed from making books to trying to earn out of every bet to survive so had to. Anyone trying to have a bet was laid after a cursory 'Betfair twist.' This was a deft little move where the bookie spun on one leg to have a look at the market on the exchanges on his laptop to see if he could still earn out of the bet or at least have the option to. All of a sudden in some quarters, nobody was having a bet, they were all trying to earn. At least that was the mind-set. If someone wanted a £500 bet but it meant that they could immediately earn £20 from it by laying it for themselves on the exchanges some bookies loathed to lay them.

The arbers soon found that it was almost impossible to get a bet on so pretty much stopped coming. Bookies even having genuine hedge bets with other bookies were treated with suspicion with the question 'How much are they making out of me?' rather than, 'Oh good I've laid it.' The meetings that used to be vibrant and well-attended by bookies and serious punters soon started to become unviable for all but those in the best pitches.

We were lucky because a lot of our pitches were good ones, especially in the south. We didn't feel the effects too much there but in other parts of the country started to give meetings a miss at places like Newbury and even Cheltenham, which was a financial blow. By this time the magazine that had got me into all sorts of trouble had gone. But I was still writing my betting ring reports for the Weekender concentrating on the big meetings and monthly in Racing Ahead. I was also writing for the local paper free but of course that didn't help the finances at all. I couldn't write too much about people in the Weekender. Their brief was usually the whole meeting in around 1600 words so it was hard enough to get all the betting news in, especially when you were covering the Cheltenham festival or Royal Ascot, but I had fun with the others.

For the Gazette and Racing Ahead I had a free hand to try and bring to life the characters that still made the racecourse a wonderful place to be. Neither bookmakers nor punters were safe from my observations, but in all honesty most of them loved being written about. Quite often a single incident would spark a whole article in the Gazette. For example, poor Barry Ward, who worked for my first boss Jack Lynn was forever after given the moniker 'Balertwine' after an incident involving his correct meteorological assessment of the inclement weather to come despite the sun shining gloriously at the beginning of the meeting. He had donned some industrial looking waterproofs that wouldn't have looked out of place on a Brixham trawler in January much to the mirth of observers in shirt sleeves. By the last he was the only one dry. The balertwine bit? He was asked why he had an elastic bungee holding his trousers up. He replied because he couldn't find any balertwine. He was a regular in my column.

Another totally true to life character was 'Armaloft' Alex, a lovely chap who had a sad affliction, premature celebration syndrome. If his arm went up in celebration it was like it was hitting either the stop button for the one we had backed or the turbo-boost on the nearest challenger. Time and time again a defeat was snatched from the jaws of victory as his arm went up with an 'Ei Ei' (how he spells Aye Aye, our universal cry of victory, yes weird I know) possibly with the addition of 'Not too far – insert name of jockey here' just before the beast that carried the burden of our bunce capitulated.

I say 'our' because Alex was a member of our Scoop 6 syndicate too, a keen follower of Andrew Mount's selections and our man in the know as far as Nick Williams went. Alex and I learned a serious lesson about the perils of drinking port after a party hosted by bookie Martyn (of Leicester) and Andrew Mount after they landed a touch of some proportion on Ryan Moore becoming Champion Jockey. We had all joined in on the punt, plus were keen to celebrate and toast (tea-total) Ryan because in the course of achieving his goal to become top jockey he also won the Scoop 6 bonus on Short Skirt for us.

To say the spread was lavish would be an understatement. All manner of meats as well as copious amounts of seafood including lobster. When all were filled to bursting an amazing array of cheeses were produced, and yes Ivor, they were of a tasty variety, with bottles of vintage port to wash them down. Now to be perfectly honest, none of it was needed. We had eaten our fill and overindulged with booze already but Andrew, Alex and I for some weird reason conjured up in our booze-addled brains that the cheese and port presented itself as a challenge to be met. There was simply too much of it for us to have risen sufficiently to it but we had a bloody good go.

Alex and I were sharing a room. I woke to the sound of a window being wrestled with followed by Armaloft launching half of his body out of it before most of last night's over-indulgences into the bushes, and luckily we were on the ground floor. I rarely have felt so ill due to booze in my life. I think I can say the same for Alex, that most hideous debilitating nauseous cranial throbbing hangover ever, richly deserved of course. The trouble was we were in Leicester where we had headed after Hereford the previous afternoon.

I had to get back to Devon and Alex to Poole via the train. I was taking him to the station. We hung around in the room until the cleaners were banging on the door. As we were laid there starfished both got texts simultaneously, Andrew with the day's tips. You had to take your hat off to the man, he had consumed the same as us. Sort of spurred on we galvanised ourselves into action and exited the room. Anyone who saw us might have wondered what the heck was going on, a driver green to the gills driving a strapping six-footer looking even greener leaning out of the window slightly more than was good for him.

It didn't help that I had no sat-nav and neither of us knew the whereabouts of the railway station. A couple of vomit deposits dotted the circumnavigations of Leicester's one way system before Alex was dropped off. After that merciful deposit I put my head down in determined fashion for one of the worst drives home ever. Incidentally, one of the horses Andrew put up that morning was an ante-post winner for the following Cheltenham.

Others who figured were a group of lads who were self-proclaimed 'Professional Punters.' In reality one of them was and still is, Slim Steve who used to help one of the old-time professionals stick on in the days before the betting exchanges. He appeared to be doing OK but you knew for sure when he had lost. Others who used to hang in a gaggle around him were probably best described as aspiring professionals. They were a mix of fantasists, students and rich kids who were no doubt black sheep and being allowed to play out their dreams. They appeared to have developed their own language where horses were described as voles and certain trainers, pumpkins. They doubtless had boundless enthusiasm for the game and a fair bit of knowledge but as to their aspiration to bet for a living, the jury was out.

One of the guys was very keen on country fashions. He would turn up dressed like a young gentleman in his last year at Cirencester Agricultural College. He talked very big but we often laid him £2 bets and then watched him jump up and down on the spot like an African warrior when the race got exciting. His cohorts had noticed this too but their comparison was more antipodean and nick-named him Skippy. He is now a fully qualified accountant, not turf. The rest of the pro-punters have gone on the missing list, except Slim Steve who is still rucking around the rings, especially point to points and making it pay.

Despite the rich tapestry of humanity keeping the colour and life in the ring things were still going downhill for the bookmakers. The already mentioned recent ruling that rails bookmakers could display prices made a whole swathe of the betting ring unworkable overnight. This was catastrophic for those layers who had invested heavily in pitches. Some were facing ruin with positions that would have been thought of as investments when purchased were now worth a fraction of their auction price and in the worst cases nothing. Those firms that had been used to betting in poor pitches and had been thrown a lifeline by the exchanges found themselves out in the cold worse than ever before. The reasons were, the boards on rails, front row layers pricing up immediately after the previous race to very small margins based on exchange prices and lack of hedge money in the ring.

Because of the advance in software and wireless Internet it was now a case that everyone with virtually no exception used the exchanges to a certain extent. There was no longer a need to have studied the form yourself, employ a card-marker to do it, or just have an eagle-eyed floorman to price up a race. Firms were just doing so by looking at the 100% books on offer, minus 5% commission, to put up a first show. This was a very precarious activity early on because quite often the markets were based around very small amounts of money. Firms offering 9/2 because there was £40 available at a fraction better and being asked for £400 either caught colds on a regular basis or quickly learnt a deft version of the 'Betfair Twist' and a thick skin.

Telling a punter that he couldn't have the bet, even though the price was there on the board, because it was gone on the machine and thus the layer was unable to hedge the man's bet with an unknown, unlicensed amateur 'bookmaker' who could well be in the Far East, didn't go down well. The past, only a few months before, where a bet was one between two gentlemen or ladies appeared to be long gone. The new attitude was totally alien to most of the old school, the old school was virtually everyone.

Other knock-on affects were, those well-informed layers who used to get their cards marked or put on bets for big owners and trainers or took money out of un-fancied horses for them, increasingly found themselves no longer needed. The middleman part they played in these transactions was a very porous link. Everyone knew that the leak was not able to be plugged with connections being able to conduct their own business with no need to let the enemy, and let's face it, that's what they always were, and only begrudgingly used, in on it. Some of these firms found playing on a level playing field a difficult transition and had to either leave by the back door with their money or tone down their game.

With off-course money not flooding into the ring, arbers not being laid, big punters getting on with no knock-backs at better odds on the machine and cash punters being bluffed on a regular basis the on-course market was being strangled from within. Rings that had been full rather than empty became less and less vibrant midweek as bookies and punters stayed away in their droves.

It was no longer plausible for many firms to continue working the racecourses as their living. The machine had made the floorman obsolete. If it was there on the machine it was there in the ring, simple. My firm had even started to miss meetings out and it soon became uncomfortably apparent that they were going to some courses just because they knew I had a mortgage to pay. Business as it was it was neither sitting well with me nor going to be sustainable too long. My time working in the betting ring was coming to a very sad but inevitable end, my last day's work on the stool was at Wincanton in February 2008.

These days I am lucky enough to still be a regular on racecourses combining my writing and PR work with a job on the other side of the fence. The sad decline in the betting rings at midweek meetings has continued. There appears to be no coming back. Many of the old-school bookmakers have retired or only turn up on busy days and festivals. The guys who have managed to keep a regular toe-hold on the tracks are largely all doing the same thing, trying to bet over-round on every race and in some cases every bet. The tail wags the dog totally with prices all changing like a relentless tide back and forth with the ebbs and flows of the moves on the machine. The hustle and bustle of the ring has largely gone.

The tic-tac man was always going to be the first to go when the ring started to utilise walkie-talkies and later mobile phones. The clerk with his pencil and gravity-defying fag ash was another certainty for extinction with the advent of computers. Floormen very rarely run around wild-eyed trying to hedge a bet at a rapidly disappearing price knowing full well to go back with nothing would result in a monumental bollocking. Even hedging in the ring had its days numbered. There is hedging, more than ever before but rather than pumping like life-blood around the ring it is being jettisoned into cyberspace ironically discarding the medium, the fabric that keeps it alive in a suicidal manner.

The salvation for the betting ring is that racing is still as popular as ever. Crowds for Saturdays, evening meetings, the summer festivals and the mighty Goliath that is Cheltenham's March meeting are up and up. Like the rains falling on seemingly barren deserts the betting rings suddenly bloom. The old names that used to proliferate show the world that they are still active; joints are polished and proudly displayed in their rightful places on the front row. The characters are still there, the colourful guys who still like to stick their necks out and attempt to raise the hackles of the punters by goading them in.

The old faces that used to be seen daily are welcome sights once more, older and craggier but like the desert fauna that bloom with abandon knowing that their window of life is an already determined brief one. The buzz is still there, some of the old 'beards' make an appearance. People attract people. Atmosphere pumps the blood. The old calls come out. There is even the odd back bet, a layer may well take a chance and fill the hod on a short one despite what the machine says. Big meetings in the UK are still a joy to behold these days. Go racing, get into the betting ring and absorb the atmosphere because at the moment at least, in doing so you are diving headlong into a glorious past of racecourse history. Back in time to a wonderful heady Technicolor world that I was lucky enough to work in and enjoy in the last two decades it existed.

The ring is not dead, just in hibernation for most

meetings of the year. Go on, go and wake it up.

*Simon Nott*